Praise for *How We Learn to Be Brave*

"With clarity, conviction, and a sure sense of the perils and the possibilities of the human condition, Bishop Mariann Budde has given us a great gift: a book that explores how God's children can stand up for the principles of His kingdom in a frail and fallen world. Courage, it has been said, is the most important virtue since it guarantees all the others, and Bishop Budde's searching account of her struggle to be brave is itself an act to be admired and absorbed."

—Jon Meacham, author of *The Soul of America* and *And There Was Light*

"'Hope,' St. Augustine said, 'has two beautiful daughters. Their names are anger and courage; anger at the way things are, and courage to see that they do not remain the way they are.' In her timely book, Bishop Mariann Budde offers hard-learned, excellent guidelines for helping not just individuals but congregations and communities learn about bravery and courage, especially in times of polarization and transition."

—The Rev. Dr. Nancy Jo Kemper, executive director (1991–2009),
Kentucky Council of Churches, and interim senior minister,
First Christian Church, Paris, Kentucky

"Few people are willing to step into those decisive moments when their voices are needed most. Bishop Mariann Budde is one of those few. Here she shares her very human struggle to find the bravery and courage required to step into life's decisive moments. She does this so to inspire others to find their own. This book is itself a gift of brave and courageous leadership."

—The Very Rev. Kelly Brown Douglas, author of
Resurrection Hope: A Future Where Black Lives Matter

"Bishop Mariann Budde weaves themes of family life, scripture, and service into a journey of bravery that you do not want to miss. Get on board for a captivating excursion through a carefully woven tapestry of ideas, prayers, meditations, and suggestions for courageous action."

—Edward W. Beal, MD, clinical professor of psychiatry,
Georgetown University School of Medicine, and author of
War Stories from the Forgotten Soldiers

"Written with resolute purpose and vitality, this marvelous book illumines the dialectical dilemma facing those who see themselves as being both in the world, but not of the world, as well as both 'children of light' and 'children of darkness.' It challenges our moral complacency in a self-obsessed secular society."

—Eric L. Motley, PhD, former executive vice president, the Aspen Institute

"By sharing with us the very realistic trials and challenges of being brave, Bishop Mariann Budde also points us along the path of growing in one of the most crucial virtues of our day. My friend Mariann inspires me. And her book will inspire you to stand up for the right and the true when it really counts."

—Jake Owensby, bishop of the Episcopal Diocese of western Louisiana, chancellor of the University of the South, and author of *Looking for God in Messy Places*

"One of the clarion voices of our time . . . Bishop Mariann Budde shows that we all have the courage to be great within us. Using vulnerability, deep insight, and enlightened spirituality, Bishop Budde invites us all to turn our decisive decisions into moments of profound meaning. This book will change many lives."

—Bruce Feiler, *New York Times* bestselling author of *Life Is in the Transitions* and *Walking the Bible*

"I need people who challenge me to see the world around me from a different perspective. In her uniquely humble way, Bishop Mariann Budde does that for me. I know she wants the best for me even when she disagrees with me. I've learned that understanding and embracing our convictions points us to our purpose in this world. *Our* calling is revealed. It's around those convictions and that calling that we often discover where we need to be brave. If you are a person of influence, you need to read *How We Learn to Be Brave*."

—Tony Morgan, founder and lead strategist of The Unstuck Group and author of *The Unstuck Church*

HOW WE LEARN TO BE
BRAVE

Decisive Moments in Life and Faith

Mariann Edgar Budde

EPISCOPAL BISHOP OF WASHINGTON

AVERY

an imprint of Penguin Random House

New York

AVERY

an imprint of Penguin Random House LLC
penguinrandomhouse.com

Most Avery books are available at special quantity discounts for bulk purchase
for sales promotions, premiums, fund-raising, and educational needs.
Special books or book excerpts also can be created to fit specific needs.
For details, write SpecialMarkets@penguinrandomhouse.com.

Library of Congress Cataloging-in-Publication Data
Names: Edgar Budde, Mariann, author.
Title: How we learn to be brave: decisive moments in life and faith / Mariann Edgar Budde.
Description: 1 Edition. | New York: Avery, Penguin Random House LLC, [2023] |
Includes bibliographical references.
Identifiers: LCCN 2022034279 (print) | LCCN 2022034280 (ebook) |
ISBN 9780593539217 (hardcover) | ISBN 9780593539224 (epub)
Subjects: LCSH: Courage. | Courage—Religious aspects. | Decision making.
Classification: LCC BF575.C8 E34 2023 (print) | LCC BF575.C8 (ebook) |
DDC 179/.6—dc23/eng/20221116
LC record available at https://lccn.loc.gov/2022034279
LC ebook record available at https://lccn.loc.gov/2022034280

Page 202 constitutes an extension of this copyright page.

Printed in the United States of America
1st Printing

Book design by Laura K. Corless

To my mother, Ann, and sister, Christine,
among the bravest women I know,

and to Paul,
whose quiet strength sustains us all

Grant us wisdom, grant us courage
For the facing of this hour.

—Harry Emerson Fosdick[1]

CONTENTS

Contents

LAFAYETTE SQUARE—JUNE 1, 2020

I am the president of law and order.

—The forty-fifth president of the United States[1]

On Monday, June 1, 2020, at 7:06 p.m., the president of the United States strode defiantly across Washington, D.C.'s Lafayette Park—trailing a retinue of aides, Secret Service agents, his daughter Ivanka, the attorney general, and America's top military leaders, including the secretary of defense and the chairman of the Joint Chiefs of Staff[2]—in order to be photographed holding a Bible in front of St. John's Church, whose parish house had sustained minor fire damage during protests the previous evening.

The president had just finished a press conference in the White House Rose Garden on the importance of "law and order," during which he threatened to use military force against American citizens who had joined protests across the country in the wake of the killing of George Floyd by Minneapolis police.

To clear the president's path, the attorney general directly ordered all demonstrators removed by force from Lafayette Park in advance of the announced 7 p.m. citywide curfew. With federal agents dispersing protesters using tear gas and bully clubs, the leader of the free world walked across the park and onto the plaza in front of the historic Episcopal church, built after the War of 1812, during which the White House itself had been burned.[3]

Arriving at the entrance to the "Church of the Presidents,"[4] attended by every chief magistrate since James Madison, the president pivoted to face the bank of television cameras, holding an upside-down Holy Bible. "This is a great country," he said. After a few more photos were taken, the president turned and left, speaking to no one.

In interviews with print and television journalists throughout that evening, I mustered every ounce of authority I could claim as the Episcopal bishop of Washington. "President Trump does not speak for St. John's," I told *The Washington Post.* "We disassociate ourselves from the messages of this president and align ourselves with those seeking justice for the death of George Floyd and countless others."

On CNN I said:

> *"Let me be clear: the president just used a Bible, the most sacred text of the Judeo-Christian tradition, and one of the churches in my diocese, without permission, as a backdrop for a message antithetical to the teachings of Jesus. Everything he has said and done is to inflame violence. We need moral leadership, and he's done everything to divide us."[5]*

As microphones and cameras kept coming toward me in the days that followed, I kept repeating: the president's actions were an outrage. Because of the intensity of the horror and grief so many felt in that national moment of racial reckoning, my words carried far and wide for a short period of time. Their significance was not about St. John's Church, or about me, but what thousands needed to hear in a decisive moment for our nation.

INTRODUCTION

Once to every man and nation
Comes the moment to decide. . . .

—James Russell Lowell, 1845[1]

We all want to be brave when it counts—to be the one who steps up, leans in, and does the right thing when it matters most. We want to bring our best selves when we're called upon, to speak with clarity and conviction in a pivotal situation.

This book is about those decisive moments when we are called to act with courage and, much to our own amazement, we do.

Although the more dramatic moments seem to catch us by surprise, looking through the wider lens of our lives, we can see that the acts of bravery that astonish even us are not isolated events. In this book, I examine life through that wider lens in hope that you, reader, will realize that you have all the raw material you need to live with courage and purpose in your decisive moments, and all the moments that precede and follow them.

Decisive moments are marking events. They stand out in our memory and are what others often remember about us. We feel a rush of adrenaline, making us acutely aware of what's happening. We feel alive—so much so that the rest of our lives can feel dull and uninspired by comparison. Yet decisive moments are almost always preceded by seasons of preparation, and they are followed by an equally important season of alignment, in which we learn to live according to what the decisive moments revealed, clarified, or set in motion. How we prepare for decisive moments determines our ability to step up to them when they come, and how we live in light of our decisive moments is, in the end, what determines their significance.

There have been many decisive moments in my life, but few as public as what happened on June 1, 2020. To be honest, I didn't have time to think. Urged on by horrified church colleagues who were watching the president walk to St. John's Church on live television and lighting up my phone with texts, I managed to find my voice and speak.

The president's actions touched a societal nerve, as did my speaking out against them. It seemed to others that I was being very brave. In truth, it felt more like being summoned to take my place alongside others who were being brave. Something had to be said, not just about that presidential moment, but the moment we were in as a nation, mourning the murder of George Floyd, watching crowds pour into the streets in cities across the nation, and facing yet again the need for racial reckoning. Because of my position, I had an opportunity to speak and be heard.

The capacity to respond in such a moment doesn't drop from the sky, nor is its significance measured by a week's worth of media coverage. Moments like these are preceded by seasons of preparation, practice, and intention, of making countless daily decisions that determine our capacity to be brave when called upon or when we're summoned not of our own choosing. Its ultimate significance is determined by how we live after the moment passes.

The more personally decisive moment for me in that dramatic week took place a few days after President Trump's infamous photo-op. I was back on what is now called Black Lives Matter Plaza in front of St. John's Church, listening to the words of the Reverend Dr. William J. Barber II. Bishop Barber is cochair of the Poor People's Campaign, a broad-based effort to mobilize low-income people of all races and their allies to create a more just society. Bishop Barber looked out on the wonderfully multiracial, intergenerational crowd gathered that Sunday afternoon and said, "Do not let anyone tell you that this is the first time people of different races, classes, and educational backgrounds have come together to fight for a common cause. It has always been such a coalition of the faithful that has brought about change in this country—Black, white, and brown; rich and poor; young and old. Everyone is needed; everyone has a part to play and an offering to make."[2]

As he spoke, the weight I had been carrying all week fell off my shoulders, and in that moment, I knew my place in the larger struggle for justice. I heard myself say to God and to the universe, "I want to be among the coalition of the faithful. I want to be among those working for the change we need now." That's the decision with which I need to align my life every day. It wasn't a new thought for me, but I felt it in a new way. It won't always burn in my heart the way it did that week, but I don't want to forget it. Like everyone else, I need grace, courage, and perseverance to be true to my decisive moment after the passion fades.

As decisive as that week was for many of us as Americans, and a marking series of events for us as a nation, it would be a mistake to conclude that all decisive moments are as public. Indeed, most of the defining moments of life never make the news cycle. It's critically important not to become accustomed to the spotlight of an audience in such moments and confuse the short-lived attention of others for the kind of change our decisive moments invite us to embrace. Most decisive moments are personal, some are private, yet all are the moments that shape our lives and make us the people we are and who God calls us to become.

Decisive moments involve conscious choice, impressing their importance upon us as we experience them, for we know that we're choosing a specific path of potential consequence. In a decisive moment, no matter how we got there, we no longer see ourselves as being acted upon by the slings and arrows of fortune or fate, but as ones with agency. We're not on autopilot; we're not half-engaged. We are, as they say, all in, shapers of our destiny, and cocreators with God. For as the word itself suggests, in a *decisive* moment, we *decide*.

This book explores a range of decisive moments that we experience in life to better understand their significance, learn what they have to teach us, and discern how to live according to the light they provide. As a person of faith, I see God at work in these moments and every moment that precedes and follows. Drawing upon examples from my own life, from scripture, and from history and culture, I hope to underscore both the universality of these experiences and the particular call to which each one of us must respond when our decisive moments come.

I am convinced that we all have the capacity to live within a narrative of great adventure, no matter our life circumstances. The courage to be brave when it matters most requires a lifetime of small decisions that set us on a path of self-awareness, attentiveness, and willingness to risk failure for what we believe is right. It is also a profoundly spiritual experience, one in which we feel a part of something larger than ourselves and guided, somehow, by a larger Spirit at work in the world and in us. Decisive moments make believers out of everyone, for no matter what name we give to it, the inexplicable, unmerited experience of a power greater than our own working through us is real. The audacious truth is that we matter in the realization of all that is good and noble and true. I want to expand our notion of what constitutes a decisive moment, for they come in many forms and require a wide range of decisions, equally decisive yet different in their energy and outcome.

In these pages, I also pay homage to the long stretches of life when nothing decisive seems to be happening and explore what happens after a decisive moment, as we live out the implications of decisions that set us on a particular course. This includes acceptance of the entirely predictable and emotionally unsettling experience of emptiness when the decisive moment passes. This is when we learn to place the intensity of a given moment within the arc of a lifetime and trust that most of life is lived in smaller acts of faithfulness. Only then can we cultivate the hidden virtue of perseverance to keep going when the going is hard.

Every moment in life is in some way decisive, part of the one life we are given to live. Recognizing life's ebb and flow helps us prepare for those moments when something important is on the line. "For everything there is a season," scripture teaches us, "and a time for every matter under heaven."[3] It takes courage to accept and fully live the lives we have been given.

In the first chapter I explore what is arguably the most dramatic and visible decisive moment, when we *decide to go,* to leave one place or way of being ourselves and move toward another. This is the stuff of heroic journey and self-differentiation. In Chapter Two, I move to the opposite end of the experiential spectrum to explore the equally heroic yet unnoticed moment when we *decide to stay,* when we choose to go deeper into the commitments we've made. Chapter Three's focus is when we *decide to start* a long process or journey toward a vision that will take years to accomplish. Whatever vision we've been given drives us to start, to take the first steps, and it helps keep us going toward the realization of a dream.

In Chapter Four, I turn to the decisive moments born of suffering, when we *decide to accept what we did not choose* and experience personal transformation through sacrificial love. Chapter Five explores the moments that come seemingly unannounced as an opportunity or summons and we *decide to step up to the plate,* whether we feel prepared for that moment or not. Chapters Six and Seven take up the emotional terrain that surrounds our decisive moments: *the inevitable letdown that follows* and *the importance of perseverance.* Indeed, without perseverance, our decisive moments would have little transformative power.

Some of our decisive moments require action; others, acceptance. Some are dramatic and there for all the world to see; others are internal, known only to the self and to God. Ultimately, what I want to communicate in these pages is that heroic possibilities lie within each of us; that the inexplicable, unmerited experience of God's power working through us is real; and that we matter in the realization of all that is good and noble and true. We can learn to be brave.

HOW WE LEARN
TO BE BRAVE

CHAPTER ONE

Deciding to Go

*Now the Lord said to Abram, "Go from your country
and your kindred and your father's house
to the land that I will show you."*

—Genesis 12:1

We learn who we are and our place in the world by telling stories. There is none more familiar or beloved than the hero's journey, the tale of one who bravely decides to go into the unknown. It is a universal narrative, spanning time and culture.[1] Yet as the spiritual writer Henri Nouwen once observed, "the most personal is the most universal, the most hidden is the most public, and the most solitary is the most communal."[2] Hearing another person's courageous journey, we can't help but consider our own.

When we are the ones to feel the summons to go, the experience sears our consciousness, marking a definitive moment in the story of our lives. It's understandable if we hesitate, for the decision to go necessarily involves leaving one place for another, releasing familiar relationships for those unknown, all in service to an enormous task that is only ours to accomplish. The risks are many, and the cost is high. Yet somehow, we are convinced that such personal sacrifice is necessary to fulfill a destiny that lies beyond our sight.

The journey begins long before we take the first step, with an inner stirring, a precipitating event, or an invitation that catches us by surprise. We feel summoned to go beyond the borders of life as we know it. There is almost always resistance, if not from ourselves, then from those who want us to stay where we are. Complete readiness is rare. Like fledglings that need to be pushed out of the nest, we often don't know we have wings until we're forced to fly.

When I was a junior in high school, my family life fell apart. It was never strong to begin with, and part of me knew the fall was coming. But I had learned to compartmentalize my emotions and keep the pervading sense of dread at bay. I was acclimated to the constant anxiety about money, lack of affection, and periodic blowups, followed by stretches of uneasy quiet that allowed me to focus my energies elsewhere.

Then the day came when my father took me aside to say that he was leaving my stepmother. I was welcome to come with him, he said, and I'm pretty sure that he expected me to say yes. He didn't mention my younger half brother, Jim, only eight years old at the time. I wasn't surprised. In the mostly silent war between our parents, our father saw me as his ally, while my stepmother fiercely claimed her son. Assuming my collusion, he asked me to keep his plan between us. I reluctantly agreed, not knowing that he had already called a moving company. My stepmother would learn of his decision a few days later when she came home from work to a half-empty house.

I don't remember how I told him, but there was no way I was going anywhere with my father alone. I didn't know then what clinical depression was, or alcoholism for that matter, but I saw their manifestations in him. His sense of intimacy with me was pure fantasy and more than a little frightening. Staying with my stepmother wasn't an option either, although I think that she, too, imagined I would. But I had lived most of my life afraid of her disdain. By the time I was seventeen I had given up trying to please her, which did not increase her affection for me, although we managed a mostly peaceful coexistence. When I told her that I wasn't going to stay with her, she insisted that I move out immediately, which was fine with me. The prospect of freedom from living under her roof eclipsed the regret I felt at the prospect of abandoning my brother.

I knew that I had to go, and I knew where.

My mother lived in New Jersey, where she had raised my older sister, Christine, and me until we went to live with our father and stepmother in Colorado. The story of our parents' divorce when I was an infant and subsequent custody battle when I was eleven is painful and messy. In the latter, I played a significant role in both the pain and the mess. When our father made a move to gain custody of Christine, I didn't want to be left behind. When we met with a family judge in his chambers, she remained uncharacteristically quiet while I exaggerated stories of our life in New Jersey, thinking how that would please our father. He was indeed pleased when the judge awarded him custody of us both, citing what I said as a determining factor in his decision. Our mother was shattered, as she had been years before by the divorce.

Looking back, I'm stunned by my capacity for cruelty. Why did I say those things to hurt our mother? I knew that she loved us. What I remember was the panic I felt when Christine spoke of moving to Colorado. I was weary of looking into the windows of other families, wondering what it would be like to belong to them. Our mother was gone a lot, working full-time while going back to school to earn accreditation in her field of physical therapy. Only later did I realize how focused she was on our survival and how alone she was in her grief. In an era when all my friends seemed to have intact families, I hated the word I barely understood and always had to explain—*divorced*. Our dad, stepmother, and new baby brother seemed to offer the normality I craved.

It was an illusion. Our time in Colorado was rocky from the start. Within months, Christine's life spun out of control, and after two tumultuous years, she left home for good. Our father tried his hand at several business ventures and failed at them all, eventually declaring bankruptcy and consoling himself with bourbon, as our stepmother frantically tried to make ends meet and protect her son. Their marriage deteriorated.

By the end of my sophomore year in high school, I had disengaged from the drama and created an alternative family with a small circle of friends. They were Christians, and to my quiet amazement, so was I. Together we attended Young Life, a gathering of Christian teenagers that met weekly at our music teacher's house. At that teacher's invitation, we joined a touring choir, and some of us began attending the church that sponsored it. Outside of family, life continued to get better. The boy up the street whom I had not-so-secretly adored finally took note of me. I discovered another home in the high school music department, and in the fall of my junior year, I was cast as Nellie Cohan in our high school production of *George M.* I knew, at last, what it felt like to belong.

When my family in Colorado collapsed, it broke my heart to consider leaving all that gave meaning and joy to my life. I was grateful that I had a mother to return to; nonetheless, I felt as if I was standing at the edge of a cliff. I felt the weight of the choice I was making, and that it was mine to make. At the same time, I had the sense that the decision was being made for me. The decision-maker, however, wasn't any of the authority figures in my life. Most of them wanted to help me finish high school in Colorado, including my church's pastor and his wife, who invited me to live with them. For the first time I can remember, I heard what I have come to identify as the voice of God speaking directly to my heart, even though my heart desperately wanted a different word.

I left on my own terms. That meant staying in Colorado long enough to perform in the musical and say goodbye to my friends, some of whom had begun their first year of college. I accepted the pastor's invitation and moved in with his family for two months, itself an education of a lifetime. I managed to complete the fall semester.

Time ran out before I was ready. The musical was over. My friends and I spent our last days pledging loyalty to one another that I knew wouldn't last. When I said goodbye to my stepmother and brother, Jim wouldn't look at me or let me hug him. My father invited me to dinner in his basement apartment, and we ate his specialty at the time—elbow macaroni with Velveeta cheese and hot dogs. On the night before my flight, my boyfriend and I sat across from each other in a restaurant neither one of us could afford and tried to be upbeat. In the morning, my friends drove me to the airport. They escorted me to the gate and onto the tarmac, gave me a bouquet of flowers, and waved as I climbed the stairs. From my window seat, I watched them walk away and then cried all the way to New Jersey.

I didn't know then Eleanor Roosevelt's definition of courage: *doing what you think you cannot do.* But that's what I did, with no illusion that what lay ahead would be easy. I felt completely alone, and yet not alone, guided in the decision that wasn't exactly mine, but that nonetheless I chose. It felt a bit like a lifesaving amputation—cutting off a cherished part of me to survive.

Returning to live with my mother would require some sort of reckoning. Although my pastor back in Colorado fretted that I would "backslide" if I returned to the Episcopal Church of my childhood, I had no such worries. In fact, I was relieved to be released from a version of Christianity that I had secretly questioned more each day.

Looking back, it's easy to see how what felt like a singular, dramatic decision had been in the making for some time. The painstaking process of emotionally separating myself from my father and stepmother enabled me, at that critical moment, to stand up for myself. The genuine affection that I experienced among my friends was healing and emboldening, yet I knew that I didn't belong with them or to them in a permanent way.

Equally significant, my mother had become a steady source of support. From the beginning of our separation at the start of those middle school years, she telephoned every Sunday evening. For years, our conversations were brief and awkward, yet she persisted in love. I could tell that she was growing surer of herself, more relaxed and grounded in her profession and in her faith. She had become more involved in the Episcopal Church that we had attended together, and there she found both inspiration and community. I don't remember how I asked if I could return to her, only that when the subject came up, it was easily settled between us.

In the end, what most prepared me for this decisive moment was the growing tension I felt about the Christian faith. I never doubted the reality of God or the presence of Jesus in my life. I didn't question the sincerity of the people in my church. They were kind, loving, and dedicated to their Lord. It was the rigidity of their belief system that I struggled with, and their certainty that God's unconditional love was only extended to those who accepted Jesus as their personal savior in the precise way they did. There was no room for deviation of experience or difference in understanding. Nor was there any place to acknowledge the ongoing struggles of human sin and brokenness that persisted after being saved. There certainly wasn't room for doubt.

I'm not sure how I would have resolved that tension had I stayed in Colorado. As with my family, I felt increasingly at odds with the spiritual authorities of my life. Leaving the church that had nurtured me felt like an act of rebellion, but I knew that I was being faithful to God in a way that I hadn't experienced before. The dissonance wasn't lost on me. I felt no need to judge or criticize my church, and yet I knew that I didn't fit in their world. I was grateful for what they had given me, but I silently rejected most of what they taught. It was the first time it dawned on me that a relationship with God isn't defined by "correct" beliefs but rather a willingness to trust and step out in faith. Without realizing it, I left Colorado in search of a more expansive understanding of God. As grace would have it, I found what I didn't know I was looking for in the Episcopal Church of my childhood.

It's been more than forty years since I stepped onto that airplane in Colorado. In ways large and small, I am who I am today in large part because I found within myself, or was given, the courage to go. Going allowed me to enjoy the stability of a loving parent; explore and deepen a life of faith within the contexts of a generous, expressive Christianity; and make my way into the world, stumbling as I went, armed with a searing experience of what it feels like to trust the promptings within my soul.

Not everything resulting from that decision was positive. In going, I abandoned my younger brother and then made promises to him that I couldn't keep, from which our relationship never fully recovered. There were other wounds from that time that took years to heal. I have learned that every decision, even the most life-affirming, carries the weight of adverse consequences. All I knew then was that there were reasons beyond my understanding for me to go, and that my life depended on taking the first steps toward a future that I could not see.

I remember as if it were yesterday, every emotion, thought, and physical sensation. Although I have had other significant leave-taking experiences, this is the one imprinted in my psyche. Leaving the life I had worked so hard to craft remains my touchstone for what a decisive moment feels like. When asked to speak of such moments, as I was during the COVID-19 summer of 2020, it is always the first to come to mind.

Four months into pandemic lockdown, Rabbi Bruce Lustig of Washington Hebrew Congregation invited me to be part of a virtual interfaith panel with the author Bruce Feiler. We were to discuss Feiler's most recent book, *Life Is in the Transitions: Mastering Change at Any Age.*[3] Having read and admired Feiler's work, I gladly agreed.

Feiler's thesis is simple: life transitions are not nearly as linear or predictable as typically described in modern psychology and self-help books. They come at any time, often when we least expect them, and we learn to take them in stride. What he calls a "lifequake" is a transition of such magnitude that it fundamentally changes our meaning, purpose, or direction. Over a lifetime, we may undergo dozens of transitions, but only a few rise to the intensity of a lifequake. During a lifequake, we are acutely aware that something big is happening, yet it takes time for us to grasp and accept that there is no going back.

All of us on the panel marveled at the prescience of Feiler's book on navigating change, released at the beginning of a global pandemic, an economic disruption, and a long-overdue societal reckoning with racism. We reflected upon all that had happened in such a short period of time and the uncertain future ahead. Amid the grief and loss, we took heart in the resilience of the human spirit and referenced our respective faith traditions as sources of wisdom and strength.

In closing, Feiler asked each of us to speak about a lifequake from our past. There was a long silence. Taking a breath, I went first and told the story of how at age seventeen I felt called to leave the life I loved. As soon as I started speaking, I wished that I had thought of a more grown-up example to share among such seasoned leaders. But after I finished, another panelist told a "deciding to go" story from adolescence. Then another. And another. Mine was not the only wavering voice.

One person who spoke that night was Imam Mohamed Magid, executive imam of the All Dulles Area Muslim Society (ADAMS) Center in Sterling, Virginia. An internationally acclaimed leader in the Muslim world, Imam Magid is a respected voice in interfaith efforts to counter religious extremism in the Washington, D.C., region. The Imam shared what it was like for him to come to America as a young man with his father, a renowned religious leader in Sudan, who was in urgent need of medical care. The young Mohamed was in awe of the doctors he met. "Some were Jewish," he said. "Others were Christian. And it didn't matter to them that my father was Muslim! They cared for him as they would their own father." Seeing such kindness and concern from those whom he had been raised to fear and distrust led him to his vocation and commitment to interfaith understanding and religious tolerance.

The last panelist to speak was my colleague and friend Rabbi Lustig, senior rabbi of the Washington Hebrew Congregation. He told of a formative experience prompted by a decision to study in Israel. He had always struggled academically, managing to pass from one grade to another on his quick wit and charm. In Israel, Bruce could no longer hide. There he was diagnosed with severe dyslexia—a devastating blow, for he feared that his exposed disability would keep him from realizing his dream of becoming a rabbi. One of his professors in Israel, himself a lifelong stutterer, promised to see him through. "Now I'm the rabbi," Bruce said, "that always makes sure that children with disabilities can have their bat or bar mitzvah."

The next day Bruce Feiler emailed to thank us. "I was especially struck," he wrote, "by the similarity of your answers surrounding the pivotal moments of your youth and calling. One after the other, you described a defining experience in your own young adulthood involving family and vocation. The collective similarity affected every listener in a powerful way."

Together we also gave witness to a lesson embedded in the stories of our common scriptural tradition, that breakthroughs in life and faith can occur when we relinquish what is familiar and go toward the unknown. We represented the three world religions that claim Abraham, a nomadic tribal leader of the ancient world, as their spiritual ancestor. More than four thousand years ago, Abraham heard a voice inside telling him to leave his home and settle in a new land. There he would become the father of a nation. So central is his story to Judaism, Christianity, and Islam that together they are known as the Abrahamic faiths.

The biblical narrative begins in Genesis with archetypal stories of how God created the universe and of humankind's fall from grace. Adam and Eve, Noah's ark, Cain and Abel, the Tower of Babel—they all have a universal perspective, for all peoples of the earth. Then in Genesis, chapter 12, the focus abruptly shifts to one couple, Abraham and Sarah, whose journey marks the birth of a new people called and set apart by God.

About Abraham and Sarah, the biblical scholar Walter Brueggemann writes: "The one who calls the worlds into being now makes a second call. The call is specific, addressed to aged Abraham and to barren Sarah. The purpose of the call is to fashion an alternative community in a world gone awry, to embody in human history the power of blessing."[4] The decisive moment is in Abraham and Sarah's response, about which the biblical account could not be more succinct:

> *Now the Lord said to Abram, "Go from your country and your kindred and your father's house to the land that I will show you. I will make of you a great nation, and I will bless you, and make your name great, so that you will be a blessing. I will bless those who bless you, . . . and in you all the families of the earth shall be blessed."* So Abram went, as the Lord had told him *[emphasis added].*[5]

There is no description of inner turmoil or doubt, no wrestling with angels or demons, no arguing with God. The childless and elderly Abram, later given the name Abraham, has a vision that involves bearing children, a promise so outlandish that Sarah laughs in disbelief when she hears it for herself.[6] Still, she joins him.

Given the matter-of-fact description of Abraham and Sarah's decision to go, it's easy to miss its significance. Abraham simply does what the Lord commands. But as Bruce Feiler observes in an earlier book devoted to Abraham, "Abraham doesn't believe in God; he *believes* God. He doesn't ask for proof; he provides the proof."[7]

Their journey has twists and turns born of human frailty and political conflict. Both Abraham and Sarah make dreadful decisions and cause harm to those closest to them. Yet their mistakes and moral failings do not negate God's promise, nor diminish the significance of that first decisive moment when they said yes. In the call, God takes their humanity into account.

Never do we feel more alive than when we, like Abraham and Sarah, take a leap of faith. Their story can be a spiritual template for us, to help us trust those rare experiences of clarity when they come. The fact that the text doesn't tell us what Abraham and Sarah felt is a helpful reminder that in our decisive moments, our feelings—or anyone else's—are surprisingly irrelevant. What matters is whether we choose to heed the call.

Deciding to go is the first step in our own hero's journey. Joseph Campbell, the comparative religion scholar whose work popularized the phrase, assures us the hero's journey is not meant for the few. "Heroes have a thousand faces,"[8] he writes, and one of them is ours. Yet reasons to stay put abound because the loss involved in leaving is so great. In the strongest possible religious language to describe what's at stake, Campbell writes, "To evolve out of a position of psychological immaturity to the courage of self-responsibility and assurance requires a death and resurrection."[9] A part of us dies in the going, for we must relinquish a past version of ourselves to become the person waiting for us on the other side.

In classic coming-of-age stories, the first step is often in response to situations beyond the hero's control. Think of Dorothy in *The Wizard of Oz* blown out of Kansas by a tornado. At first, most young heroes resist the call and only reluctantly consent later. In *The Lord of the Rings*, Frodo wishes that the evil One Ring had never come to him. Sometimes the journey begins with liberation, as it does for Harry Potter, freed from the miseries of 4 Privet Drive when he steps on the train bound for Hogwarts. Along the way, our heroes meet significant mentors, cross important thresholds, experience great trials, and have at least one transformative crisis. Sometimes they go on to new lands, while at other times they return home with wisdom to impart. The hero's journey is both intensely personal, the foundation of a life distinctly and meaningfully lived, and of communal importance, for the call is never for self alone. The effects of a courageous, faithful life reverberate across time and space.

Understandably, the first decisions to go, typically in adolescence or young adulthood, stand out in our memory as critical markers in the inner work of identity formation and self-differentiation. Their significance grows over time, however, as they become our personal archetype, the recognizable pattern of what happens to us when the call to go comes around again, which it does throughout life. The heroic journey beckons more than once.

When I was relatively new to my vocation, I struck up a conversation with another Episcopal priest who served as the director of a camp and retreat center. He seemed much older than I and contentedly settled in his life. Yet as we chatted, I learned that he was leaving his position to become a counselor in a residential program for adolescent felons. The joy and excitement in his voice were palpable as he said something I've never forgotten: "I feel as if I have been preparing my entire life for this job."

In one sentence, he was telling me a lot—certainly about his passion and repertoire of gifts, and perhaps of his own adolescence. His new position was not a step up any ladder of vocational advancement; in fact, it had more in common with what Henri Nouwen referred to as "downward mobility."[10] But something stirred in me as this seasoned priest spoke. What a thrill it would be to have such a sense of purpose, such a coming together of failings and strength, suffering and resilience. I knew that there is no way to fake that kind of clarity, nor leapfrog over years of hard work to get there. It would require a lifetime of faithful steps, of answering one call and then another and then another, until by grace one reaches the kind of integration and opportunity summed up by the words, *I have been preparing my entire life for this.*

———

In 1943, such a moment came for Black American pastor and educator Howard Thurman when he was invited to go to San Francisco to co-lead a newly forming interracial Christian community. As he would later write, the invitation "kindled in my mind the *possibility* that this may be *the* opportunity toward which my life has been moving."[11]

Thurman had been among the first Black Americans to cross the color line in numerous religious and academic institutions in the Jim Crow era. He was a sought-after preacher in both Black and white churches and a frequent speaker at religious conferences, although often denied service at the hotels where they took place. Over the years, he grew increasingly impatient with American Christianity's unwillingness to confront racism within its churches and society at large. He drew a distinction between what he called the "genius of the religion of Jesus" and the practice of Christianity as he had experienced it in the United States.

Thurman had long recognized what the call to go felt like and what it could make possible, even in seemingly impossible circumstances. Born in 1899, he grew up in the segregated city of Daytona, Florida. His father died when he was seven, and as all Black children were and are, he was forced to navigate the evils of racism at an early age. Yet he was blessed to be raised by loving adults and nurtured in a protective church community. His elementary school teachers recognized his intelligence and helped him continue his education beyond seventh grade, when public school for Black American children ended. These positive influences instilled in him, as he would later write, a strong sense that his life and what he did with it mattered.[12]

In childhood and adolescence, Thurman found solace and strength in nature, inspiration from his family and teachers, and a fierce desire to study—forces that enabled him to overcome innumerable obstacles. At every step, his singular focus, obvious brilliance, and personal sacrifice, aided by the sacrifices others willingly made on his behalf, gave him a sense of life purpose and responsibility. He also found benefactors, lasting friendships, and spiritual mentors across the racial divide intended to keep whites and Blacks "separated by a wall of quiet hostility and overt suspicion."[13]

Thurman experienced grace—mystical encounters mediated through the natural world or the kindness of strangers—that persuaded him that God had something to do with the doors that had opened for him at opportune moments. His biographer Peter Eisenstadt writes, "Providence would be perhaps too strong a word for Thurman's belief; luck is too weak. It was one of those uncanny linkages between two events, a moment when a hidden, benign undergirding and connectedness of the universe is glimpsed."[14] That sense of God's presence gave Thurman the courage to accept what life gave him as his fate and make it his destiny.[15]

A foreshadow to the call to go to San Francisco occurred ten years earlier while he was on pilgrimage in India. Thurman and his wife, Susan Bailey Thurman, were leading a delegation of Black Americans on a mission of friendship organized by the World Student Christian Federation. Mahatma Gandhi's nonviolent movement against British colonial rule had captured the world's attention. Their three-hour conversation confirmed Thurman's conviction that nonviolence was the only way to overcome racial injustice in the United States. "It may be through the Negroes," Gandhi said to Thurman as his parting blessing and exhortation, "that the unadulterated message of nonviolence will be delivered to the world."[16]

While on a sightseeing visit to the Khyber Pass, part of the ancient trade route through a rugged mountain range between modern-day Afghanistan and Pakistan that enabled the exchange of ideas, culture, and faiths from many lands, Thurman was given a vision: "to create a religious fellowship that was capable of cutting across all racial barriers."[17] For years after, he held close the prospect of establishing a truly interracial expression of Christianity that would celebrate the wondrous diversity of humankind. When the invitation came a decade later to create such a church in San Francisco, "I felt a touch on my shoulder," he wrote, "that was one with the creative encounter of the Khyber Pass dream."[18]

Thurman's decision to leave an esteemed position at Howard University, the flagship academic institution for Black Americans, to start an interracial church puzzled those around him. Howard's dean pressed him to consider the risks he was taking, not only for himself but also for his family. Thurman wrote to his counterpart in San Francisco, "There are risks involved in our bold venture and we must be prepared to take our share of them."[19] This was his chance to create a church that was worthy of Jesus. "Thurman had been living within the confines and constraints of his fate, the accidents of his birth and upbringing, since his earliest days," Eisenstadt writes. "The San Francisco church was an opportunity to seek and claim his destiny."[20]

There was nothing easy in the work to establish what became the Fellowship Church. Yet Thurman never expected ease, and for another ten years he poured everything he had into the church. It was a time of fulfillment and frustration. It was a time of satisfaction with the church's influential ministry in San Francisco and disappointment that it didn't have the national impact he had hoped. It was a time of intense focus on pastoring a relatively small congregation and when he published his most influential book, *Jesus and the Disinherited*.

Thurman would hear the call to go once more, in 1953, to assume a tenured leadership position at Boston University, a historically white institution. He left reluctantly, for he considered Fellowship

Church the most significant accomplishment of his life. Yet he also felt a responsibility to rising generations and was persuaded that a university would offer the widest possible platform for his message of nonviolent resistance. It was at Boston University where a young doctoral student named Martin Luther King Jr. first encountered Thurman, who would remain his spiritual inspiration for life.

Whether for the first or the hundredth time, in choosing to go, we feel as if our lives matter. When we go in fear, we are given the courage to do what we think we cannot do. When we go in excitement, it's as if we had been preparing our whole lives for this moment. That the cost of going is high merely confirms the importance of the call.

Years ago, a good friend heard the call to change professions in midlife. Her new vocation would require significant education, with a corresponding loss of income. It would also involve moving, with or without her family, to another city for a year of on-site learning. The resistance to this call, both within and around her, was intense. Even after she made the decision, she wavered for more than a year. It was an agonizing time, as she held both the call and all that worked against it.

Then one day, something shifted inside her, and she was clear in a way that she hadn't felt before. She continued to be gracious and considerate of her family, but she no longer doubted that it was time to go. When I asked her about the change, she simply said, "I knew that it was time. It's not going to be easy, but not going simply wasn't an option." The decisive moment had come.

Such clarity, when and however it comes, is a gift. It first came to me at age seventeen. I can count on one hand the times I have felt it, but thanks to the psychic imprint of that initial experience, and aided by examples of courage found in scripture, history, and literature, and in the lives of those I've met, when the heroic journey presents itself, I recognize it and know what to do. I believe that we all do.

CHAPTER TWO

Deciding to Stay

Here I stand, I can do no other, so help me God.

−Martin Luther[1]

Ian Bedloe is the seventeen-year-old protagonist of Anne Tyler's 1991 novel, *Saint Maybe*. He blames himself for the apparent suicide death of his older brother, Danny, and subsequent family tragedies. One evening, as he wanders the streets of his home city of Baltimore, Ian sees a neon sign in a storefront window, "Church of the Second Chance." He takes his place among a small group of wounded souls, and he hears himself telling them of his brother's death and of his guilt. The minister, Reverend Emmett, a kind yet spiritually uncompromising young man, assures Ian that forgiveness is possible, provided that he atones for his sins. So Ian decides to drop out of school and take a menial job to help provide for his brother's children. Years go by as he goes to work each day, cares for his family, and is a faithful member of the church. Still, the forgiveness that he longs for eludes him, and he begins to question the choices he has made.

Sensing that Ian is troubled, Reverend Emmett offers to walk him home from church one Sunday afternoon. As they walk, all of Ian's frustrations pour out of him. "I feel like I'm wasting my life!" he cries. Reverend Emmett stops and turns to look directly into Ian's eyes. "This *is* your life," he says softly. "Lean into it. View your burden as a gift. It's the theme that has been given you to work with. This is the only life you'll have."[2]

Given the drama, adrenaline, and outward energy involved in deciding to go, staying put can feel like being trapped. Yet the decision to stay also can be brave and consequential. Making that choice, particularly when there are compelling reasons to leave, involves a similar internal struggle and building sense of crisis, leading to a decisive moment, as strong as the decision to go. But there the similarity ends, for in deciding to stay, we choose to go deeper into the life we already have.

Because the call to go is rightfully associated with the adventurous side of courage, choosing to stay can appear as if we are settling for less. Yet depth, which is the fruit of stability, is essential to a mature life and our capacity to make a lasting difference in the lives of others. In choosing to stay, we acknowledge that there is more at stake than what we feel or want. We learn that there is more than one way to live a brave life and that some of the most courageous decisions we make are ones that no one sees.

I first read *Saint Maybe* at a time when I, not much older than Ian, was struggling with what it meant to stay in my own life. Reverend

Emmett's words to Ian felt like God's words to me: "This *is* your life. Stay where you are."

Until then, my life had been largely defined by going—moving from one place to the next, stepping out of one world and into another, learning to be brave in face of the unknown. Now I was in my early thirties, married, with a three-year-old and a newborn, working full-time at a job that I was supposed to love. I did love it much of the time, and I loved much of my life, which made it hard to acknowledge or talk about how I felt. Driving the streets of Toledo, Ohio, I would sing along with a Nanci Griffith song playing on the radio. I'm *working on a morning flight to anywhere but here*, wishing it were true.

I see now that my internal struggle was a call to accept and experience the gift and the cost of stability. It has been a recurring theme, whenever I wrestle with the call to stay. I've had to learn, time and again, that faithfulness isn't always about taking big leaps, but also walking with small steps, and that it's possible to make a lasting difference in the world by tending to one small corner of it.

A foreshadow of this realization came in our first year of marriage, which my husband, Paul, and I spent in Honduras, working in a school for impoverished children. Initially it seemed as if we had made an enormous commitment. As our time there drew to a close, however, I realized that those who dedicate their *lives* to serve in that way are the ones who are able to have a transformative impact for good. I returned to the United States wanting to be that kind of person, but also sensing that nothing in my life had prepared me for the discipline it would require.

Marriage, parenting, and parish ministry became my teachers, each representing a small world for which I was responsible, each valuing stability over change and constancy over the excitement I craved. Not knowing who to talk to, I found solace and guidance in books. Bits of wisdom would come to me, keeping me grounded when I wanted to fly.

The summer our elder son, Amos, was a toddler, we traveled with him to Sweden, joining my mother on her annual trek home. We stayed at the rustic farm that her parents bought after World War II and where my Swedish family gathers in the warmer months. It's a beautiful spot, and we were welcomed warmly. Yet within a week, I felt characteristically restless, wanting to travel the country, hike for hours, cross over to Denmark, and tour other parts of Europe. Instead, every day Amos and I walked down a dirt path to watch the neighbor's sheep graze. He would stand there for what felt like hours, and I stood next to him, trying to fight off the envy I felt for those with untethered lives. When he napped, I buried myself in books, desperate in my attempt to stay connected to the wider world. Looking back, I wish I could reassure my younger self that the world wasn't going anywhere, but at the time, I couldn't shake the feeling that I was missing something, and possibly even failing at whatever I was supposed to be doing with my life.

That summer I stumbled upon *The Little Prince* by Antoine de Saint-Exupéry. It's a whimsical story, written in the style of a children's book, filled with wisdom about the foibles of human nature. The Little Prince rules on a small planet known as Asteroid 325. On that planet there also lives a single rose, which the Little Prince loves yet causes him all manner of grief with her pretentiousness and need for constant affection. To cure his wounded heart, the Little Prince decides to leave his rose and travel the galaxy.

After he lands on Earth, the Little Prince climbs a mountain so that he might get a better view. From the top he sees hundreds of roses in a garden, a revelation that causes him to sit down and weep. His rose had assured him that she was special and that it was a privilege to love her. But here in one garden alone there are hundreds just like her. If she is but an ordinary rose, who, then, is he?

Then the Little Prince meets a fox who teaches him an invaluable lesson. "To me," the fox says, "you are nothing more than a little boy who is just like a thousand other little boys. I have no need of you. And you have no need of me. I am just a fox, like a hundred thousand other foxes. But if you tame me, then we shall need each other. To me, you will be unique in all the world, and I will be the same for you."

The Little Prince realizes that the same is true about the roses in the garden. For all their beauty, he does not love them. He loves the single rose on his tiny planet that he had watered and sheltered and cared for. "It is the time you have wasted for your rose that makes her so important," the fox tells the Little Prince. "You are responsible for your rose."[3]

Picturing our son as my rose, I knew with unmistakable clarity where my heart and responsibility lay. I also realized that if I didn't rise to this kind of singular love, all my longed-for adventures and efforts to make a lasting contribution would mean nothing. "You are responsible for your rose" has become a mantra, reminding me of the sacredness of all the people entrusted to my care.

The Presbyterian minister Frederick Buechner likewise taught me, and countless others, the value of stability. Through his memoirs and other writings, he helped me want to be a person upon whom others could depend and to relish the days when nothing important seems to be happening. Buechner writes,

> *If I were called upon to state in a few words the essence of everything I was trying to say both as a novelist and a preacher it would be this: Listen to your life. See it for the fathomless mystery that it is. In the boredom and pain of it no less than in the excitement and gladness: touch, taste and smell your way to the holy and hidden heart of it because in the last analysis all moments are key moments, and life itself is grace.[4]*

That was the summer I began listening as hard as I could, learning day by day what it meant to be, as the Psalmist writes, "like trees planted by streams of water, which yield their fruit in its season, and their leaves do not wither."[5] It has become a lifelong practice, one that requires constant renewal, as the days spent in place far outnumber those when we're called to go. There is nothing complacent in choosing to stay, and the faithfulness required is, indeed, heroic.

Still another writer who encouraged me on the staying path is the Benedictine nun Joan Chittister. I have kept one of her books, *The Rule of Benedict: Insights for the Ages*, close by since it first fell into my hands years ago. Benedict established a monastic community in the tumultuous years of the fourth century, when the world seemed to be falling apart. He was grounded in the simple practices of daily life and the grace to be found in a healthy balance between work, prayer, study, and rest. Chittister, publishing in the 1990s, brings contemporary language to Benedict's rule. "Life is a teacher of universal truths," she writes. "To the wise, life is not a series of events to be controlled. Life is a way of walking through the universe whole and holy."[6]

Reading *The Rule of Benedict* over the years has given me wisdom and grace to reorient my focus on where I am rather than where I think I want to go. One sentence leapt out when I first read it and remains with me still: "It may be the neighborhood we live in rather than the neighborhood we want that will really make human beings out of us."[7] I sometimes hear in prayer or meditation an invitation to substitute the word *neighborhood* with whatever it is I'm struggling with, and its truth resounds. Where I am may, in fact, be where I need to be. What I want, although perhaps good and admirable, may not be possible or worth the cost.

In no way do I mean to suggest that staying in abusive or harmful situations is God's will, or that self-sacrifice is always the path of love. Pursuing our heart's desires can be the most life-affirming choice we can make, even when it takes us from other commitments. What I am saying, however, is that in the course of a well-lived life, we also need sufficient groundedness to develop deep relationships and to discover often-hidden treasures of longevity. There is a different kind of joy in being the one whom others can count on.

Even now, as my caregiving responsibilities have shifted to my mother, on the other end of the life cycle, Chittister, Buechner, the Little Prince, and Ian Bedloe remind me of the importance of daily faithfulness, and that sometimes the most loving and courageous decision is to stay where we are.

For all the goodness of staying, however, there are times when it isn't something we choose but rather must accept as the fruit of disappointment. When a door of opportunity closes, there is no denying that staying feels like failure. Yet such disappointments are unavoidable in life, and after a necessary season of grief, the time given to us to stay is often when seeds of new possibilities are planted and slowly take root. If we're not going anywhere, there is time and opportunity to tend to our character and hone our skills, to savor grace in small packages, and to learn perseverance.

In 2002, I experienced a disappointment in my vocation that set me back for more than a year. I was in my tenth year at St. John's Episcopal Church in Minneapolis, Minnesota, and had enjoyed some success in my role. People around the country had begun contacting me, asking if I might consider a new position. I, too, was pondering what might be next. The possibility of becoming dean of an Episcopal cathedral was something I dreamed of, to lead a church with a broad civic vision. The dean of the cathedral in Minneapolis offered to mentor me, so that I might become a strong candidate for another cathedral when the opportunity arose.

Then, without warning, word came from the bishop's office that our dean had resigned. Rumors swirled. There were hints of scandal, but nothing was made public. It was a destabilizing event in our diocese, and yet I knew immediately that I would apply to succeed him. It was an audacious ambition, and the timing was awkward. It also felt like an opportunity I couldn't let pass by.

The search process for a new dean was uneasy from the beginning, complicated by dynamics in our family, at St. John's (located only few miles from the cathedral), and in the wider diocese. I was initially rejected by the search committee, which was both devastating and humiliating, but then a few weeks later the search committee invited me back as a finalist. It was obvious to all involved that I was the token woman on the slate and the only local candidate. I almost said no, but I knew that I would regret not trying. And for a brief window of time, it seemed as if momentum was in my favor. I remember saying to God in prayer that for all the ambiguity around me, if I were called, I would gladly dedicate the rest of my vocational life there.

In the end, the cathedral chose someone else. Knowing from the beginning that I was a long shot, I still wasn't prepared for what happened next. Although managing to put up a good front and be publicly supportive of the cathedral and its new dean, whenever I was alone, I couldn't stop crying. My body seemed to fall apart, and I entered a long season of chronic pain. My family life suffered, as Paul and our young sons didn't know how to respond to my grief. Life in the diocese was also in turmoil, and I felt adrift in the congregation I had served so long. I lost confidence in the bishop's leadership, and feeling betrayed, he lost faith in mine. Someone on his staff pointedly suggested that I look for work in another diocese.

Sometime within that year of grief, to my surprise, a new call to stay slowly took root in my heart. It didn't take away the sorrow I felt but seemed to come up alongside it. I recognized the feeling of clarity that I had known other times when the call was to go. As the prospect of staying grew stronger, so did my excitement. With a sense of alignment with those closest to me, I cherished the prospect of allowing both our sons to graduate from high school and Paul's professional life to flourish, while going deeper in ministry in the church I had served for a decade.

I spoke first with those closest to me—my husband and a few friends. Then I asked the St. John's leadership how they would feel if I publicly committed to stay for five more years. If I stayed, I told them, I would need to learn new skills for the work ahead. St. John's had grown in the ten years we'd been together, and the congregation needed a new kind of leader. If I was to be that leader, the changes before us would need to be as dramatic as if I had left and they called a new priest. On the other hand, we had the foundation of our ten years together upon which to be brave.

The leadership accepted my proposal. Although I had warned them of the changes to come, neither they nor I knew exactly what that meant. In truth, the years that followed were not easy; in fact, they were among the most challenging of my time at St. John's. They were also the most fruitful. I learned that choosing to stay didn't mean staying the *same*. I wound up staying for eight more years.

At best, the decision to stay is a daily choice to remain wholeheartedly in one's life and commitments, resisting the temptation to drift, passively disengage, or stoically soldier on. The times of crisis come after seasons of doubt, disillusion, or boredom, when we find ourselves wishing for any other life but ours. At the crossroads, it takes courage to choose *either* to leave *or* to stay with a deeper understanding of what staying demands or makes possible.

A story in the Gospel of John speaks powerfully to that crucible moment. It tells of a time when Jesus' teaching has become increasingly controversial, and the crowds that once hung on his every word begin to fall away. Even some of those closest to him no longer want to be part of his movement. "This teaching is difficult," they say, "who can accept it?" In a moment of sober assessment, Jesus turns to the twelve disciples of his innermost circle and asks, "Do you also wish to go away?" His question hangs in the air. At last Simon Peter speaks up: "Lord, to whom would we go? You have the words of eternal life."[8] They had come too far to turn back now. Their destinies are bound up in his.

The decision to stay with Jesus when others choose to leave is one that I turn to often in my own life, as a leader of a Christian denomination experiencing significant numerical decline. Knowing our failings all too well, I can easily understand why so many choose to leave the church and the faith. What convinces any of us to stay within our faith tradition when new insights and personal maturation cause us to question what we had once accepted as true, or when spiritual leaders or entire communities fail us? What keeps our faith from growing stale and increasingly irrelevant?[9] Time and again I have found my answer in Simon Peter's question: *To whom would I go?* I've come too far with Jesus to walk away. Although I am often discouraged by my own failings and those of others, I've never lost faith in Jesus, and I am forever inspired by those who live their lives by his light and strive to be more like them. And so I stay.

One inspiration is the Reverend Dr. Kelly Brown Douglas, the inaugural dean of the Episcopal Divinity School at Union Theological Seminary and Canon Theologian at Washington National Cathedral. Douglas is the author of six books, all written from a womanist perspective, a disciplined approach to theology that prioritizes the experience and perspectives of Black women. Her work is both rigorously academic and deeply personal, as she shares her struggles to remain a Christian given the real harm done to Black people, both historically and in our time, by those who purport to follow Jesus.

Taken as a whole, Douglas's writings tell of her circular spiritual journey, in which she will come to a settled place, and even peace, in her decision to stay in the church, only to have the question resurface, as one student pointedly asked her, "How can you, a Black woman, possibly be a Christian, when Christianity so often contributes to your oppression?"[10] Every time a new version of Jesus' question "Do you also wish to go away?" confronts her, Douglas's response is to write, delving further into the history of white supremacy and the spiritual strength of her ancestors. Thus far, every time she has come to the brink of walking away, to my astonishment and gratitude, she chooses to stay.

As a child, Douglas attended the only Black Episcopal church in Dayton, Ohio. She loved church, and she especially loved hearing stories about Jesus. As she ventured beyond her congregation in adolescence, she was surprised to learn that not only were there white Episcopalians but that the church was *predominantly* white. (Later, asked about her choice to remain in a church so enmeshed with white supremacy, she chuckled as she remembered thinking, *What are all these white people doing in my church?*)

Growing up, Douglas listened to her parents talk in hushed tones about racial violence. She once asked her father what had Black people done to make white people hate them. By the time she reached college, she realized that the problem of white hatred didn't lie with Black people, but within those determined to hate. She resolved to find some way to dedicate her life to dismantling what

W.E.B. Dubois called the "color line" that perpetuated racial violence and consigned so many Black children to poverty. In college,
she also experienced her first crisis of faith, as she realized that she
had grown up with an image of Jesus as a white man. "How could a
White Jesus ever care about me," she asked herself, "not to speak of
caring for poor Black children? And how could I, a Black person,
ever have faith in a White Jesus?"[11]

It was Douglas's college chaplain, David Woodyard, who introduced her to the writings of Black liberation theologian James
Cone. Cone's critique of white Christianity became a spiritual lifeline. Here was someone, within the church, naming the horrific
realities of white Christianity's complicity with slavery and all its
evils. Cone posited the liberating image of Jesus as the Black Christ,
one in solidarity with oppressed peoples of the earth. "When I read
Cone's words," Douglas recounts, "my questions were answered. I
could be Black with a love for Jesus without contradiction, because
in fact Jesus was Black like me. As Cone made clear, Jesus, born in
poverty, was one with all those Black children who were trapped
behind the life-draining color line of inner-city realities."[12] Cone's
theology gave Douglas renewed appreciation for the faith passed
down to her. Douglas would go on to expand the horizons of Black
theology with a focus on the experience of Black women in white
society and LGBTQ+ persons in the Black Church.

But the cost of remaining a Christian, and a Black leader in a
predominantly white denomination, is high. In her most recent
book, *Resurrection Hope: A Future Where Black Lives Matter*, Douglas
acknowledges that once again, she is experiencing a crisis of faith,
perhaps the most significant of her life. Her sober conclusion is that

whiteness has so corrupted the moral imagination of American society that it can no longer envision a world where Black lives truly matter.[13] Yet she is adamant, as Cone was before her, that white Christianity in both its historical and present contexts is an anathema to the mission of Jesus. She reserves her harshest critique for Christians who were or are proud supporters of white supremacist causes, but she is equally uncompromising in her assessment of "good" white Christian leaders, who have the privilege of selective response to issues of injustice.

When her own son asked her how she can persevere in hope, she answered by telling him about his great-great-great-grandmother. "Every time I think about Mama Mary, I think of those Black people who were born into slavery, died in slavery, and never drew a free breath. In fact, they never dreamt that they would ever breathe a free breath. Yet, they fought for freedom anyhow.... When I think of them and their fight for freedom, I cannot give in to that which would destroy Black life."[14]

Douglas believes that Jesus, as in the incarnation of God in human life, continues to experience the realities of crucifixion in the lives of Black people and feels the pain of it as if for the first time. She walks with him to the cross. But she also finds hope in his resurrection—the same hope that her forebears clung to and that she is determined to carry forth.

I feel the gift of her challenge daily, one that doesn't allow me to forget the wider implications of a faith that is not only personal, but collective; that has something to say about the societal wrongs that as a white Christian I don't always see. As a colleague and friend, scholar and preacher, Kelly Brown Douglas will not stand silent when I miss the truths that are obvious to her. More than once, in response to some societal outrage against Black people, she has called me to say, "Mariann, we have to *do* something, *say* something." She chooses, at huge cost to herself, to stay in a church where leaders like me need her continued prodding. We owe her more than words can convey, for the integrity of our witness is at stake.

There is undeniably a sacrificial component in the decision to stay, a sense of loss for the roads not taken and the weight of burdens that we choose not to lay down. Staying can be also a loving gift to ourselves and others. For in choosing stability in one area of our lives, we give those who depend on us an opportunity to thrive and grow. We don't typically associate stability with sacrificial love, for there is nothing visibly heroic about it, but beneath the surface, there is another story to be told.

In no relationship is such sacrifice more necessary than in a marriage or similar lifelong commitment. I have witnessed evolution of divorce from the scandal I experienced as a child to a common family configuration. As a priest, I have presided at dozens of weddings and then later counseled many of the same couples when they decided to separate. I've walked with friends and family members through the poignant, traumatic process of parting. Thus, I marvel all the more at the resilience of long-term marriages. I am blessed to be in one myself and I know something of the cost. At several junctures, Paul and I made the conscious choice to stay married. It wasn't a given that we would.

As with the call to go when I sensed God was leading me toward new horizons, I've had experiences throughout our marriage when the call was equally clear to stay. Paradoxically, that clarity often came through what I *didn't* hear. In the times when we seriously considered ending our marriage, or at least separating indefinitely, my prayer was for clarity. If I was going to be the one to act on a decision that would forever change our lives and adversely affect the lives of many we loved, I needed a *definitive* word, an internal assurance that leaving was the path to take. Not hearing it, I stayed. Thankfully, so did Paul.

Considerable societal forces work against long-term commitments, and there are long stretches when the private side of marriage is surprisingly lonely. Although in some circumstances, divorce is the most life-giving choice, the rewards that come through perseverance in marriage are many. Through challenge and sacrifice, we grow in our capacity to forgive, to accept, and to prize the uniqueness of another human being. Over time, we realize the privilege and responsibility of playing a supporting role in another person's life story. There is also the shared story of a marriage, the emotional space created between the two in which others can find welcome and sanctuary. A good marriage becomes solid ground upon which others can build their lives, and for us, the outward dimension of married life has been a source of deep joy. Paul and I have been enriched by sharing our lives and our home with others, and we both cherish the opportunity to be there for both loved ones and strangers during their crucible moments.

I have always been fascinated with public marriages in which both partners share a vocation. That was especially true for the presidential couple who led our nation through the Great Depression and World War II, Franklin and Eleanor Roosevelt. In a time of unrest and suffering, Franklin and Eleanor were icons of stability, compassion, and courage. The country looked to them for strength, not knowing that there was a private side to this iconic marriage that never would have survived the tabloid press of today, or that it had nearly ended in divorce twenty years before they entered the White House. Given the circumstances and social mores of their time and class, such a scandal would likely have derailed Franklin's political career long before he was a candidate for president. Eleanor chose to stay. It's impossible to imagine what the nation, and the world, would be like today had she chosen otherwise.[15]

Eleanor had accepted the marriage proposal of her distant cousin in 1905, when she was nineteen years old. Franklin already had political ambitions, and Eleanor longed to be of service for good in the world. At the turn of the new century, each saw the world as both perilous and full of promise. Some historians describe their first years of marriage in glowing terms,[16] yet others suggest that the couple struggled from the beginning. In his biography *Eleanor*, David Michaelis writes that as early as their honeymoon, they established what would become a pattern—Eleanor retreating into long, stony silences while Franklin openly flirted with other women.[17] "Yet the more disappointed they were with each other," Michaelis adds, "the more readily they took on the problems of the world."[18]

Soon, however, Eleanor's call to public service was submerged in the exhaustion of childbirth and parenting. Sara Roosevelt, Franklin's mother, was an overbearing presence in their household, and Eleanor assumed a subservient, almost childlike role as Franklin's career flourished. Eleanor also refused to acknowledge what had become widely known in Washington's social circles: Franklin had fallen in love with her personal secretary, Lucy Mercer. The affair went on for years. Eleanor persisted in denial, at least publicly, until a fateful night in 1918 when Franklin returned home from an extended trip to Europe. Unpacking Franklin's bags, Eleanor discovered Lucy's love letters. Years later, in private correspondence, she acknowledged that, "The bottom dropped out of my world, and I faced myself, my surroundings, and my world, honestly for the first time."[19]

While Eleanor's heart was broken, her mind was clear, and she immediately offered Franklin his freedom. Sara was mortified at the prospect of the spectacle of a divorce, and she threatened to cut off Franklin from the financial support upon which his privileged life and political future depended. In the chaotic days that followed, Franklin's closest friend and political adviser, Louis Howe, served as mediator. What began as a tentative conversation became a negotiation of marital terms. Sara was distraught, Franklin sulked, and Eleanor remained calm. She would not stay in a marriage where she was not wanted.

Although Franklin left no known public or private record of his true feelings, his biographers describe Lucy Mercer as the love of his life. Nonetheless, his love for politics and public service proved greater, and he broke off their relationship. He apologized to Eleanor and vowed never to see Lucy again. It was a promise he did not keep, but they were apart long enough for Franklin and Eleanor to find their way.

In choosing to stay, Eleanor redefined what it meant for her to be Franklin's wife. She insisted on separate bedrooms and having full authority of their household. She fired all the servants who were subservient to Sara and hired people loyal to her instead. Biographer Blanche Wiesen Cook writes, "As Eleanor waited for her heart to heal, a new resolve emerged, in the shape of words that were to be the banner of her adult life, words she repeated as advice to her many friends and the young people who would from then on enter her world, a new world of action of activism: 'The life you live is your own.'"[20] Eleanor no longer expected or even wanted sexual intimacy with Franklin, but she needed assurance that he genuinely wanted her as his life partner.

Indeed, Franklin would soon need Eleanor more than anyone could have predicted. In the summer of 1921, he contracted polio. In the first touch-and-go weeks of high fever and agonizing pain, Eleanor never left his side. As Franklin inched toward partial recovery and eventually came to terms with permanent paralysis, Eleanor and Howe were united in their determination to keep his aspirations alive. Eleanor realized that without a future in politics, Franklin would give up altogether. She believed in that future, and that she belonged beside him.

By the time Franklin was elected president in 1932, their outwardly focused marriage was firmly established, their partnership, based not on intimacy, but on shared values, mutual need, and affection.[21] They also established their own communities of support—men and women who tended to their emotional and physical needs while they served the nation. Historian Doris Kearns Goodwin likens the Roosevelt White House to a small hotel. Some houseguests stayed for years, including Franklin's and Eleanor's intimate partners. Others came for days or weeks, including heads of state, family members, and political advisers. In this way, Goodwin writes, "the extended White House family permitted Franklin and Eleanor to heal, or at least conceal, the incompletions of their marriage. . . . There were areas of estrangement, untended needs that only others could fill."[22] Although rumors abounded, the media protected their private lives.

Eleanor traveled on Franklin's behalf, spoke for him at events he could not attend, and returned with reports of what she had witnessed. She was his most trusted adviser. Franklin encouraged Eleanor's activism and defended her against detractors when she spoke out against racial injustice and abusive labor practices. He didn't seem bothered by the intensity of her friendships and romantic relationships with either men or women. She, in turn, accepted and even befriended the women who tended to Franklin's personal and intimate needs.

I have long pondered the cost and consequences of Eleanor's decision to stay, and what became for her a powerful moment of self-differentiation. Yes, she would stay married, but not as before. She would be her husband's partner, but she also gave herself permission to seek happiness wherever she could find it. Most important, she determined what truly mattered to her, which was a life of service, committed to the ideals of justice, peace, and human rights. She prioritized showing up in racially integrated spaces and befriending those working for civil rights. Among the thousands for whom a word of encouragement from Eleanor Roosevelt gave them courage and inspiration was Howard Thurman. In 1944, she was the keynote speaker for his send-off when he left Washington, D.C., for San Francisco, and she was among the first to sign a commitment card for his interracial church.[23]

Most decisions to stay are less widely consequential than Eleanor Roosevelt's or Kelly Brown Douglas's, but the impact of our choices may reach further than we will ever know. Choosing to stay is rarely recognized for the heroic journey it can be, and few may see the depth of crisis we experience as our lives hang in the balance. It is, by and large, an inner struggle. That may be for the best, for what we need most of all is time and space to reflect and a willingness to trust our inner compass. Even in situations that we desperately want to leave, we may well come to the astonishing realization that staying is our *choice*. We are not trapped. We are agents of our destiny.

There is no manual to consult or blueprint to follow in these crucible times. But there are paths of wisdom that come to us in literature and in our faith traditions. And we learn from the courage of others. Most important is the discerning of our hearts, for each of us must come to our own decision. Whether or not we consciously call upon God, it is a holy journey. We are wrestling with profound questions of identity and relationship, the purpose of our lives, and the sacrificial nature of love. There is nothing passive or inconsequential in choosing to stay. With it paradoxically comes an invitation to start something new. To that new beginning, we now turn.

CHAPTER THREE

Deciding to Start

A journey of a thousand miles begins with a single step.
—Laozi, Dao De Jing[4]

It is surprisingly easy to read all the biblical accounts of Jesus' life and miss his most decisive moments. Of the four Gospel writers, Matthew, Mark, Luke, and John, only Luke mentions it, almost in passing. Yet this is the moment when Jesus embarks on the journey leading to his death—and he knows it.

Previously, Jesus had stayed close to the villages in northern Israel surrounding a large lake known as the Sea of Galilee. His hometown of Nazareth served as base camp for an itinerant ministry of teaching, healing, and feeding the impoverished communities of subsistence farmers and fishermen. In the rabbinic tradition of ancient Judaism, he had gathered a small group of disciples who traveled with him.

One day Jesus takes a break from his ministry to climb a nearby mountain. It was his custom to slip away periodically from the crowds that followed him everywhere, often at night, sometimes for an entire day. For Jesus, climbing mountains was a form of prayer. Hiking cleared his mind, and the views gave him perspective as he cast his gaze toward the horizon. He typically went alone, but this time he invites three of his closest disciples—James, John, and Simon Peter—to join him.

All four gospels mention this particular climb, which New Testament scholars agree gives the story both historical and theological significance. On the mountaintop, Jesus has a mystical experience in the form of a conversation with his spiritual ancestors, Moses and Elijah. His disciples watch as a light comes upon him that seems to change his appearance, and they hear the voice of God speak from a cloud: "This is my Son, my Chosen; listen to him!"[2] For reasons they don't understand at the time, Jesus swears them to silence.

The whirlwind of human need awaits Jesus when he descends from the mountain. Before he has a chance to catch his breath, he's back at work. But something is different. Whatever Jesus experienced when the light shone and the voice from the cloud spoke, he is now clear that his death is imminent. In this knowledge, Jesus makes the pivotal decision to go where all the prophets before him went to die. "When the days drew near for him to be taken up," Luke tells us, "he set his face to go to Jerusalem."[3]

In the seventy-eight miles from Galilee to Jerusalem, Jesus' ministry looks much the same as before. He teaches and heals people. He tells some of his most memorable parables on the road, including the story of the Good Samaritan and the Prodigal Son. He makes a point of traveling to areas that most Jews avoided and speaking to those deemed as outcasts of God's generous, inclusive love. He has dinner with his close friends Martha, Mary, and Lazarus and honors Mary's choice to take her place among the men rather than busy herself in the kitchen. These are the stories we remember; less so the journey during which they took place.

For Jesus, however, it is the journey that matters, its destination foremost in his mind. The only clues we're given that time is running out for him is his impatience with those still vacillating in their decision to join him, and in the way Jesus teaches his disciples along the way. There is an urgency in his tone as he repeatedly tells them that he would not be with them much longer—something they do their best to ignore.

The fact that few others realize the significance of the call to start underscores its initially private nature and how long it can be before those first stirrings are seen in light of where they ultimately lead. The first steps are typically small, and the journey is long enough that the odds of completing it are low. Moreover, not every resolve to attempt something results in a dramatic change. Those that do, however, generally trace their beginnings to a moment that hardly anyone noticed.

The decision to start has much in common with the decision to go, as it involves movement from one place to another. The difference is in the imperceptibility of the shift. There is little drama. In fact, deciding to start often requires staying where we are for a time, because of the significant preparation required to begin. We might even go backward at first, in the sense of making up for past decisions or retracing our steps to take the path we didn't choose years before.

Early in my years at St. John's, a parishioner named Cindy Dowson told me that she had decided to pursue her dream of becoming a nurse. This was a big deal because Cindy had never gone to college, and she hadn't done well in high school. When she was a teenager, Cindy's main objective was to live on her own. She waited tables at first and eventually landed an office job, where she stayed for fourteen years. She met and married her husband, Scott, and they started their family. It was after the birth of their third child and Cindy had left her job to care for their children full-time when she told me of her decision to start on the journey toward the job she had always wanted.

Starting meant taking one night class per semester at a local community college because she needed remedial and prerequisite courses before she could even apply to the nursing program. "I was so nervous driving to my first class," she remembers, "and afraid that I couldn't do the work." Caught in rush-hour traffic, she arrived late and the classroom door was locked. When the instructor opened it, he coolly informed her that he expected all his students to be on time. She was never late again.

For six years, Cindy worked slowly and steadily, one course at a time. When at last she was accepted into the nursing program, she enrolled full-time for two more years. Each day, she would rise early to study several hours before her children woke up and then return to her studies after they fell asleep at night. She remained active in our church during those years, and although we all knew that she was going to school, it was easy for us to forget what that meant for her. Only she and Scott, her stalwart supporter, knew the cost.

Cindy graduated from nursing school during the economic recession of 2009, when no hospitals were hiring. She instead took a night job as a home care nurse, caring for chronically ill children and adults. "I often felt like a glorified babysitter," she told me. "But I needed the work." Several years later, her brother-in-law mentioned that the county hospital needed nurses for their trauma units. Cindy applied the next day and was hired on the spot. "That's where I learned to be a nurse," she said, "working alongside those who care for those enduring the worst forms of suffering." A few years after that, she at last secured her dream position in obstetrics.

More than twenty years later, I asked Cindy what she remembered about the moment she decided to start on the path and where she found the courage to persevere. First, she told me about her grandfather, an endocrinologist at the Mayo Clinic, who, as a diabetic child, was one of the first to receive experimental doses of insulin. That treatment saved his life, and he resolved to pay it forward. "It had never occurred to me that I could pursue such a path," she said. "But when our son Michael was born, the memory of my grandfather came back to me, as if to encourage me to do something brave."

Another seed was planted, she said, during a class that she took at our church, offered by one of our more gifted lay leaders, Richard Howard, on discerning life purpose. "I'll never forget what it felt like," she said, "when John drew a vertical line on the white board and told us that it represented our life span. He told us to put the date of our birth at the bottom, and then to estimate the date of our death and put it at the top. Then he asked where we were on that line and what we wanted to do with the time we had left." Cindy knew her answer.

Cindy also spoke of the obstetrics nurse who was with her as she delivered their son. "She was amazing," she recalled, "so caring, encouraging, and *good* at her job. I knew that I wanted to do for other women what she did for me." The deciding factor, however, was what she had learned in parenting her children. "Given my childhood, motherhood was not a foregone conclusion," she said. "But through parenting, I learned that I am a natural caregiver. Deciding to become a nurse was an outgrowth of my being a mom."

When I asked if she had ever thought of giving up, she was quiet for a moment. "No," she said at last. "I just kept going. Of course, I was humbled by how much I had to learn. But I don't regret how long the journey took." She paused again and laughed. "I am now the matriarch of the obstetrics night shift. They call me Mama Cindy."

Each decision to start a courageous journey is unique, yet the experience is universal. When, for example, does a child decide to walk or to speak? The first stirrings are instinctive and unconscious. Still, there is agency in her decision to pull herself up and take her first steps toward her mother's outstretched arms. As she grows, choice takes on an increasingly larger role, such as when learning to ride a bicycle or play a musical instrument. Then we see even more clearly the courage required in a young person's decision to start, the risk and vulnerability of stepping beyond her current capacity to learn something new, and her excitement at accomplishing what was once impossible.

Humans are not the only species with the capacity to begin journeys of consequence. My bird-watching husband tells me of certain species that make migratory treks from one end of a continent to another. How do birds know when to start? What keeps them on course when they've not made the journey before? Where humans differ, it seems, is in our capacity to envision possibilities beyond our sight and move toward them. It isn't instinct alone that propels us. A spiritual beckoning draws us toward a destiny. But the choice is ours to make, even as we feel summoned by a presence or an energy not our own.

When we make that decision, the path ahead may be clear, as in a course of study or vocational accreditation. Others are ambiguous, more akin to driving at night in the fog, which is how the novelist E. L. Doctorow described the process of writing. "You can only see as far as your headlights," he said, "but you can make the whole trip that way."[4] In either case, whatever lies beyond the horizon can only be realized by moving toward it.

A formative decision to start came to me by surprise, shortly after I had decided to stay and fully dedicate myself at St. John's in Minneapolis. I wasn't going anywhere, yet almost immediately I had the sense that it was also time to start preparing for an unforeseeable future. I had no definitive destination or path, and surely no guaranteed outcomes, but I realized that if I ever wanted to be considered for a position of greater influence in the church or beyond, I needed to be ready when the opportunity presented itself. I wasn't sure how to go about it, only that it was critical to begin.

The first inkling of a direction came when I was invited to preach at Virginia Theological Seminary, my alma mater, and to lead a preaching class. It was an unexpected affirmation of my work beyond St. John's at a time when I was still feeling fragile after the cathedral search process. The morning of the chapel service in which I was to preach, the academic dean sat down next to me as I was finishing breakfast in the seminary dining hall. I don't remember much of our conversation except the moment when he said, "I think it's time for you to begin a Doctor of Ministry degree, and I'd like you to consider doing so here."

With his words, a door opened. Not knowing what such a course of study would entail or where it would lead, I knew that I wanted to walk through it. The following January I began my doctoral studies at Virginia, a four-year journey that afforded me a structured learning environment and a place to explore the spiritual practice of leadership. It also brought me back into conversation with leaders in the Washington, D.C., area, something that would prove important later.

I was also inspired by the courageous example of others choosing to start something new. In those years, I served as a conference leader for an organization dedicated to clergy wellness, known as CREDO (an acronym for Clergy Reflection, Education, and Discernment Opportunity). My team and I led two conferences a year for my peers across the church, guiding them through an intentional process of self-examination and visioning. At the end of each session, we gathered in a circle to allow participants to give voice to their aspirations for the future.

Here are two such stories, which I recount with permission. Ernesto Medina attended a CREDO conference I led in June 2003. At the time, he was serving as the Provost of the Episcopal Cathedral in Los Angeles. Throughout the week, Ernesto dazzled us with his creativity and exuberant spirit. He gently teased me for my serious demeanor and invited me to kick back and have fun with the group.

When it was Ernesto's turn to speak on the last day, he said, "I want to dance at my grandchild's wedding." It was a vision of joy, characteristic of his seemingly boundless jubilance, yet something in his voice caught my attention. Ernesto was exactly my age, and like me, he had two adolescent children. Grandchildren were a long way off for both of us. "Life expectancy for men like me isn't great," he said quietly. "Taking care of myself physically is a struggle. Just before I came to this conference, I was diagnosed with diabetes." He paused. "I want to do whatever it takes to be there for my kids and my grandkids."

Ruthanna Hooke was at that same conference. She had recently been hired as a homiletics professor at Virginia Theological Seminary, the first partnered LGBTQ+ person to serve on the faculty. In accepting her position, Ruthanna found herself at the center of our church's human sexuality debates, which at the time were often polarizing and mean-spirited. She did not relish the spotlight focused on her private life. Her call was to teach.

During our week together, Ruthanna allowed herself to imagine a future in which she would not be known primarily for her sexual orientation. When the time came to speak of her aspirations, she said, "I want to be recognized as the top of my field within ten years." There was a spark of determination, even defiance, in her eyes. I wanted to stand and applaud.

I have carried Ernesto and Ruthanna in my heart for more than twenty years. Their words became my own, as I savored watching our sons grow up and imagined the grandmother I would be to their children in the then-distant future. I allowed myself to acknowledge my own ambition to be a leader, with the ability to make a real difference in people's lives and the direction of our country. Ernesto and Ruthanna helped me remember that such aspirations require daily intentionality over long periods of time. I needed to start and keep moving toward my future.

As all this was stirring in my personal life, a leadership crisis in our diocese intensified. A group of us decided to organize and request a comprehensive strategic planning process to clarify collective goals so that we might invest accordingly. Feeling pressured by our actions and genuinely puzzled by our lack of support, the bishop reluctantly agreed and then promptly announced his plans for a sabbatical. The diocese hired a leadership consultant from the nearby Lutheran seminary, the Reverend Dr. Craig Van Gelder. As one of the advocates for the process, I was asked to serve on the leadership team, known as the Bishop's Commission for Mission Strategy. The irony of the name was not lost on us, for the bishop had largely absented himself from our efforts.

For more than a year, we gathered information on the state of our church and tried to make sense of it. We held listening sessions to better understand the lived experience of our people. We pored over congregational data and sober trend lines that told a story of precipitous institutional decline. We often argued among ourselves and were quick to point out the failings of others.

Dr. Van Gelder gently invited us to look at our own behavior and move beyond what he called "our culture of critique." "It takes no energy or creativity to point out what's wrong," he said. "But for everything you criticize, I challenge you to offer at least one suggestion for making it better." His words have stayed with me, as an invaluable reminder that although it is easy to find fault, the people who make a difference for good are those who work for creative solutions.

At one particularly difficult all-day meeting, we came to the sobering conclusion that the future of our diocese, and the Episcopal Church in general, was bleak, given how many congregations were struggling simply to survive. Dr. Van Gelder observed that we lacked a coherent vision or a unifying sense of identity or purpose. The implications weighed heavily on my heart. During a break, I took a walk with my friend and colleague Michele Morgan, also a member of the commission and a gifted priest who had discerned her vocation at St. John's years before. Her path to ordination and then finding work in the church had been anything but easy, but the fact that she was a priest at all was because of the Episcopal Church's movement toward full inclusion of LGBTQ+ persons. Our diocese, for all its problems, had been on the forefront of that effort.

I confided to Michele that I wasn't even sure that it mattered to God if the Episcopal Church survived. The mission of Jesus and the work of the Holy Spirit was not in question, only the relevance of our church in that work. Even if we did survive, to whom would it matter? Michele was quiet for a moment and then said, "It matters to me. This is the church that welcomed me." Her words went straight to my heart, and I thought of all the other people I loved who had found a spiritual home in the congregation I served and throughout our denomination. I realized that I was not going to give up on our church, for the sake of the people I loved and in service to the best of our tradition.

That was the day I said to God that if I were ever called to be bishop, I would give my whole heart to the work. I knew that it was what I wanted to do, and like Ruthanna, I dared to name my ambition. Our bishop announced his decision to retire later that year, and when the time came, I put my name forward to be among the candidates from which his successor would be elected.

It would be two years before the convention in which delegates from around the diocese chose the next bishop. I continued my work at St. John's, all the while preparing for what I hoped and believed would be my future. Looking back, I see more clearly what I couldn't acknowledge at the time—that I was not universally loved or respected among my peers, nor did many trust my motives. For all my preparation and sense of call, there was a quiet anxiety in the air on the day of the election among my supporters that I tried to ignore. By the end of the second round of votes, it was clear that I would not be elected. The rest of the day was a blur, as Paul whisked me out of the hotel as quickly as possible. Once again, I did my best to be gracious after not being chosen for a position to which I would have dedicated my life.

In the weeks and months that followed, I felt my world grow small. Our sons were off at college. Paul's work kept him busy. The ministry at St. John's carried on. I went through the motions of living, knowing full well that St. John's deserved more from me than I could give. When I finally told the church leaders that I didn't have a guiding vision to lead them anymore, a wise and caring woman, Kay Kramer, gently asked, "Do you have sufficient vision for a year?" I thought for a moment and answered honestly that I did. She smiled. "Then why don't we take things one year at a time for now?" I felt her blessing to lead as best I could for a window of time. But what was I to do with all the signs and aspirations that had led me to pivot toward a more influential position? It physically hurt to remember how much I had wanted to be elected bishop and at the same time how embarrassing it was to acknowledge that desire.

> *Give up all the other worlds*
> *except the one to which you belong.*[5]

This haunting line from a poem by David Whyte, "Sweet Darkness," guided me in that year when the future went dark. I stepped back from every commitment or activity outside of the realm of trusted relationships and work that was mine to do. Yet again, I was driving in the fog, unable to see past my headlights. It felt as if I were on borrowed time.

On the day the new bishop of Minnesota was ordained to his post, I took part in the service alongside my clergy colleagues. He and his family greeted me warmly, as did many others, and yet I knew that I had no place among those celebrating that day, except to be gracious. Waiting for me at home that afternoon was an email from a friend, Lisa Kimball, who had recently moved to northern Virginia to join the faculty of Virginia Theological Seminary. On that same day, she told me, the bishop of the Episcopal Diocese of Washington had announced his retirement. "Consider this," she wrote. At the time, nothing felt more unlikely than being elected bishop anywhere, much less in Washington, D.C. Yet undeniably, I felt a spark of hope, and with it, in time, permission to dream again. I didn't say a word to anyone.

It's tempting to view the decisions and events of those years through the lens of inevitability, all leading to where I am now, but as I lived them, the path was anything but certain. I could only see far enough to take the next step, and the next, and then the next. The disappointments I'd experienced caused me to doubt my inner drive, and I tried to imagine other paths I could take to live a meaningful life.

Somewhere during the two-year journey from the day I first learned that the former bishop of Washington was retiring to the day of my election, I came to accept two realities: first, that the call to dedicate my vocational life to the spiritual renewal and structural transformation of the Episcopal Church was non-negotiable, and second, that I could not know in advance the context in which I would live it. The time had come for me to leave St. John's, and should no diocese choose me as their bishop, then I would have to find another way.

When I finally told Paul of my intention to enter the Washington election, he said softly, "I don't want to see you get hurt again." "The odds are against me," I conceded. "But the opportunity is worth the risk of not being chosen." A quiet conviction stayed with me through to the election, and it has sustained me since, even during the hardest times.

I often wondered what had happened to Ernesto and Ruthanna since they declared their intentions to start toward a distant future, and I reached out to them and asked if my memory of what they had said nearly twenty years ago was accurate. Both responded immediately and said yes. Their lives had evolved in ways they could not have anticipated, yet they still remembered the decisive moments of that conference as marking events.

Ernesto went on to serve as senior pastor of the largest Lutheran church in Fremont, Nebraska—quite a distance from his life as an Episcopal priest in Los Angeles. He spoke with the same exuberance I remembered as he explained how his decision to commit to his health was part of a larger arc in his life. "My focus at the CREDO conference was on staying alive for my kids and grand-kids," he said. "But that was but one expression of a quest, begun years before and that continued in the years that followed, to do brave and bold things, to claim my identity and my gifts, and to heal from the wounds I wouldn't allow myself to acknowledge for years."

The CREDO conference helped him focus on his physical well-being, which he had long ignored. It was something that he realized could not be separated from his commitment to a larger life and sense of adventure. A few years later, Ernesto and his wife, Susan, now empty nesters, surprised everyone, including themselves, when they moved to Nebraska, where Susan found meaningful work and Ernesto took a position at the Episcopal cathedral in Omaha. Within weeks, they both realized that they had found their spiritual home in the upper Midwest. Nonetheless, Ernesto struggled vocationally, as he felt the weight of our denomination's racial inequities. Then in 2011, Ernesto was in a car accident, and during his long and painful recovery, he became severely depressed and withdrawn. A therapist helped him recognize that his exhaustion stemmed from trying to find his place in our church.

In 2016, Ernesto walked the five hundred thirty miles of the Camino de Santiago, an ancient pilgrimage route in northern

Spain—one of the many adventures on his bucket list. "I was old and fat and it was really *hard*," he said. He reached out to his family and friends back home, asking for their prayers and support. One night, he joined a small group of pilgrims sitting around a fire. The young man preparing them dinner turned to Ernesto and asked him to talk about Jesus. "I spoke from my heart," he told me. "I said that Jesus chose to love without exception, and that with this last breath, he forgave those who were killing him. I told them that I want to learn to love like that and that's why I follow him." Ernesto heard himself speak for the first time in years about his faith in ways that others could understand. "*That's* my vocation," he said, "talking about the love of Jesus to whomever I can. On the Camino, I once again found myself claiming freedom—yet another expression of fulfilling the goal to dance at my grandchildren's weddings."

Two years later Ernesto retired from the Episcopal priesthood and took an interim position in a nearby Lutheran congregation. To his astonishment, the deeply conservative Nebraska Lutherans warmly welcomed him. "I felt free to be myself in ways I never did in the Episcopal Church," he said. Then he was called to the senior pastor position he now holds. "I would never have had this opportunity in the Episcopal Church," he said ruefully. "I was always boxed in, somehow. Among the Lutherans, I'm happier than I've ever been."

Now in his sixties, Ernesto is facing health concerns again, as his diabetes continues to progress. But he's ready to take bold steps yet again. His focus isn't simply to stay alive, but to live with integrity, authenticity, and joy. "I have the greatest bucket list in the world," he said, "and I've mostly completed it. Now it's all about leaving a legacy." He paused for a moment and laughed. "But my kids will have to be more cooperative if I'm going to make it to my grandchildren's wedding. At this rate it might be their sixth-grade dance."

Unlike Ernesto's many travels and institutional changes, Ruthanna has remained at Virginia Theological Seminary. She still teaches aspiring clergy how to preach, and she is now the Associate Dean of Students. When I reminded her of her intention to be at the top of her field within ten years, she protested, "Surely I said within *twenty-five*." A decade, we agreed, seems like a long time looking ahead and far less so looking back.

The controversies of human sexuality that Ruthanna hoped to put behind her only intensified later in that summer of 2003, when the General Convention of the Episcopal Church (our highest legislative authority) consented to the election of an openly gay and partnered priest, the Reverend Gene Robinson, as bishop of the Diocese of New Hampshire. Lines were quickly drawn, and many theologically conservative bishops, priests, and congregational members either left the Episcopal Church or were determined not to abide by changes in our polity that called for the full inclusion of LGBTQ+ persons.

At Virginia Theological Seminary, some students became more strident in their protest of Ruthanna's position on the faculty while others held her up for adulation. In response to the brewing storm across the wider church, the seminary hosted a series of forums on theological and biblical arguments for and against full inclusion. Ruthanna was asked to take part in one such forum, which would be moderated by the ethics professor, and where she alone would speak alongside one of the more outspoken conservative students.

She reluctantly agreed. "All the students, faculty, and staff turned out for the event," she recalled. "I felt as if my sexuality was on trial." The cost of having to make a public defense of her right to be a professor at the seminary was almost more than she could bear.

Still, Ruthanna persevered. "The CREDO conference helped set my sights on something that truly mattered to me," she said. "I remember the feeling of empowerment, the invitation to dream big." She had come to the seminary before finishing her doctoral dissertation, the first step toward reaching her goal. But then she and her wife decided to start a family. "That really blew people's minds," she laughed. "I was forty-two at the time—a pregnant, older lesbian." Everything slowed down with the birth of their son, Silas. She didn't finish her dissertation until he turned one. She didn't start working on her first book, *Transforming Preaching*, for several years after that.

All the while, Ruthanna defined her own way of teaching how to preach, focusing on what she calls "embodiment," being fully present in one's body and using the voice's full range. It's an approach that requires vulnerability and authenticity, the willingness to be fully oneself in the pulpit. The seminary community was skeptical at first, some viewing her methods as suspect, even immoral. Yet her students responded, and in time, her classroom became a haven of depth and joy. She struggled with the dissonance between the space she was creating and the rest of the seminary. "Students would have transformative experiences in my classes, but these did not seem to shift the seminary culture as a whole," she said. "I often felt like I was speaking in a room with no resonance; there was a sense for quite a while that what I was doing did not meet with a response from the community. Thankfully, that has changed in recent years."

One decisive factor in that change has been Ruthanna's evolving understanding of what it means for her to be at the top of her field. She realized that she wanted to influence the entire seminary experience for students. Gradually, she moved toward administrative work. When the seminary rebuilt its chapel, Ruthanna became its first Associate Dean of Worship, which allowed her to establish a warmer, more inclusive tone when the community gathered for prayer. A few years later, she was promoted again, to her current position of Associate Dean of Students, which affords her considerable influence on the life and culture of the seminary.

Although Ruthanna originally resisted being the "lesbian homiletics professor," she came to realize that her sexuality was part of what she brought to leadership. "Being LGBTQ+ is all about speaking or not speaking," she said. "You can hide without speaking. But my approach to preaching is about authenticity and finding one's voice. How can I tell students that they must bring their whole selves into the pulpit and their ministries if I don't do the same?" Now, as dean of students, she "preaches" the ideal of transformational leadership, not simply in words but in the slow, steady work of systemic change.

So has she reached her dream? "Maybe I have," she said thoughtfully. "I've certainly become a leader within this institution." She continued, "I still care about my academic field, and I never want to give up teaching, but now culture change is at the heart of my vocation." She is the first to acknowledge that the seminary has a long way to go in addressing both gender dynamics and embedded racism. "But we're doing the work," she said with a tone of satisfaction. "My impact has been like leaven, slowly changing this place from within."

Leaven is an evocative metaphor for all who feel called to start a process of communal or societal transformation, because the work is largely invisible for a long time. History is full of stories, often told from the perspective of successful outcomes, that gloss over the prolonged struggle that follows a decision to start down such a path, and how often those in one generation take the vision as far as they can and then must pass it on to the next. Sometimes the next generation even undoes the hard-won accomplishments of their forebears with the pendulum swings such as we are witnessing in our time with the overturning of *Roe v. Wade* and other U.S. Supreme Court decisions. In history, as in our personal lives, there is no straight path.

Yet only when brave individuals choose to start and then persevere does society change. As but one example, it was Supreme Court Justice Thurgood Marshall's relentless quest across decades to challenge Jim Crow laws and flagrant lynching practices that, in the words of biographer Juan Williams, "guided a formerly enslaved people along the road to equal rights."[6] Marshall's tenacity and legal genius are widely known from the *Brown v. Board of Education* Supreme Court decision of 1954, which declared segregated schools unconstitutional. Faded from our collective memory is how hard he worked before *Brown v. Board* to eradicate the evils of segregation, winning the grudging respect of white judges and attorneys across the South and attaining near-godlike status in Black communities.

Marshall came from a proud lineage of enslaved and free Black people who fought against slavery, established businesses, educated their children during Reconstruction, and built homes in the newly integrated neighborhoods of Baltimore. But by the time Thurgood was born in 1908, the resurgence of white supremacist laws and policies had begun. During his childhood and adolescence, increasingly oppressive restrictions stripped Black Americans of their legal rights and access to equal housing, employment opportunities, and education. Lynching became the means of social control.

Marshall's family fought against this tide of state-sanctioned oppression and protected their children as best they could from the violence and cruelty of segregation, sending them to the best colored schools they could afford and drawing upon the resources of extended family to help them attain college educations. Still, Marshall and his classmates were keenly aware that the dominant society treated them as less worthy of educational investment than their white counterparts.

His political awakening began when he was in high school, when the principal punished him for misbehavior by giving him a copy of the U.S. Constitution and telling him to memorize it, which he proceeded to do in one afternoon. His interest slowly grew while he attended Lincoln University, a historically Black university in Pennsylvania. When he was denied admission to the University of Maryland School of Law on the basis of race, he reluctantly applied to Howard University School of Law, which he considered a far less reputable institution.

Marshall had the extraordinarily good fortune to arrive at Howard in 1929, the same year as its new dean. Charles Hamilton Houston had begun his audacious plan to make Howard a "West Point of Negro Leadership."[7] Houston's determination to raise up a generation of brilliant Black lawyers inspired Marshall. Under Houston's commanding leadership, Marshall began his lifelong journey to use the legal system to dismantle Jim Crow.

One decisive moment to start on the long road to justice came during his last year at Howard. Dean Houston had invited Marshall to join his legal defense team in the case of a Virginia Black man, George Crawford, accused of murdering two white women. Together they worked for months on Crawford's defense. Despite the lack of a weapon or witnesses linking Crawford to the crime, the all-white jury found him guilty. Yet due to the tenacity of his defense team, Crawford escaped the death penalty, which was cause for celebration. As Marshall would say later, "If you get a life term for a Negro charged with killing a white person in Virginia, you've won, because normally they were hanging them."[8]

The Crawford case, and the opportunity at age twenty-two to be in the courtroom alongside his brilliant mentor, set Marshall on a course from which he never wavered. "Marshall felt the preachers, the politicians, the businessmen, and even the civil rights leaders could talk and raise money and put stories in the newspapers," Williams writes. "But it was up to lawyers to stand up and help a black man with his life on the line."[9] Houston often told his students that they could become the architects not only of a more just legal system, but a new social order, one court case at a time. That became Marshall's purpose in life.[10]

Like other Black leaders of his generation, Marshall believed that he stood at the threshold of historical change, yet he held no illusions about the daunting task before him. Throughout the grim decades of the 1930s and '40s, Marshall traveled through the deep South, "a source of inspiration and courage," writes historian Gilbert King, "as he fought countless battles for human rights in stifling antebellum courtrooms where white supremacy ruled."[11] His tenacity and legal brilliance were evident in his arguments before the Supreme Court, and then as the first Black American to serve on the highest court of the land from 1967 to 1991.

Unlike other civil rights champions of his time, Marshall lived long enough to witness the tides of change turn once again, this time against his efforts. He grew increasingly isolated on the Supreme Court, relegated to writing dissenting opinions in case after case. In his final years, he became a recluse. Yet his legacy remains among the finest of his peers, born of his unwavering conviction that the U.S. Constitution, although not written for his people, could provide the path for their freedom; that courts of law, although often unjustly biased against them, could be the arena of justice; and that just laws could, in fact, encourage basic decency. "There is little truth to the old refrain that one cannot legislate equality," Marshall said at a White House conference in 1966. "Laws not only provide concrete benefits, but they can also even change the hearts of men."[12]

The Reverend Dr. Pauli Murray, a contemporary of Marshall's, also chose law as the best way to pursue justice for Black Americans. From an early age, she had been engaged in nearly every form of advocacy and agitation, most notably with her favorite form of protest: "confrontation by typewriter."[13] She was determined, unlike most men of her generation, including Thurgood Marshall, to include Black women in the struggle for equal rights.

Murray's life was one decisive moment after another. Her mixed-race family was a source of pride and devotion, yet mental illness and poverty loomed large. She was raised by her aunt Pauline, a teacher who encouraged her to pursue education, and despite the formidable barriers, Murray spent much of her life in academic settings, consistently at the top of the class. She was always poor, working for almost no pay as a writer, union organizer, and fundraiser, and later as an attorney. She never stayed long in any position. She struggled privately with her sexuality and gender identity until she met the love of her life, Renee Barlow, in her late forties. Murray's legal arguments, crafted in near-manic states of intense work and physical deprivation, are now part of the canon of civil rights law, yet she was never adequately compensated or recognized for her efforts.

Murray entered Howard Law School in 1941, twelve years after Thurgood Marshall. Several events had led her to conclude that law was the most effective arena in which to seek societal transformation on matters of race. But as she prepared to take her place among the aspiring lawyers at Howard, Pauli was stunned by the overwhelming gender prejudice she encountered. She had grown up surrounded by strong women, attended a women's college, been befriended by Eleanor Roosevelt, and worked in organizations where women held positions of leadership. This was the first time she experienced the full-on effects of gender discrimination. "The racial factor was removed in the intimate environment of a Negro law school dominated by men," she wrote in her memoir, "and the factor of gender was fully exposed."[14] All of her energies had previously been focused on the struggle against prejudicial laws based on race. Now in a nearly all-male Black institution she encountered what she described as the twin evils of discriminatory violence that she aptly called "Jane Crow."

That marginalization galvanized her. "Murray countered gender discrimination the same way she countered race discrimination: by trying to prove her abilities," writes Troy Saxby in *Pauli Murray: A Personal and Political Life*.[15] Another biographer, Rosalind Rosenberg, agrees that Murray's experience at Howard was the major turning point: "Murray's experience of feeling unwelcome would prove pivotal for her. From that moment, she began to think about the battle for civil rights more broadly, as a movement that should encompass attacks not only against race discrimination but also against gender discrimination."[16] It became her lifelong quest to treat both race and gender equity as non-negotiable in civil rights law and societal practice.

While still in law school, Murray first conceived of the legal arguments that would later prove decisive in the Supreme Court's 1954 decision on racial equity in *Brown v. Board of Education* and its 1971 ruling on behalf of gender equality in *Reed v. Reed*.[17] It was an audacious attack on both forms of discrimination, based on the 13th and 14th Amendments to the Constitution, which had abolished slavery and granted full citizenship to all persons born in the United States. But for generations, the Supreme Court had effectively nullified legal protections for people of color, most notably in the 1896 case *Plessy v. Ferguson*. All efforts to overturn *Plessy v. Ferguson* had thus far focused on the gross inequalities in segregated life, chipping away at racial disparities one case at a time. Murray, in contrast, became persuaded that a challenge to the inherent indignities and irreparable harm brought about by separation itself was the way forward. Segregation of the races, and of people by gender, she argued, was designed to maintain a caste system in this country.

Murray's classmates and professors initially scoffed at the notion that women be included in the legal struggle for civil rights. Nor were they persuaded that a direct attack on *Plessy v. Ferguson* was possible. But Murray persuaded her academic adviser to allow her to write her senior paper exploring such an approach. This became the foundation for later writings that would one day garner the attention of Howard Thurman, and later still Ruth Bader Ginsburg. Murray's comprehensive study on racial segregation laws throughout the South, *States' Laws on Race and Color: Studies in the Legal History of the South*, became, in Thurgood Marshall's words, "the Bible for civil rights litigators." She also consistently called male leaders to account and joined forces with the burgeoning women's movement.

Murray is a case study of a life lived ahead of her time. She laid the foundations for what was to become normative in our society. Although her personal experience was often one of failure, she took satisfaction when her ideals were vindicated. In her later years, she often said, "I have lived to see my lost causes found." One of her delayed victories has special significance for me and all women clergy: as a practicing Christian and lifelong member of the Episcopal Church, Murray actively participated in the decades-long debate to allow women's ordination. In the microcosm of our church, it was as fierce and nasty a debate as the struggle for women's rights in the wider society. In 1977, one year after the 1976 General Convention, the governing body of the Episcopal Church voted for that historic change, and Pauli Murray became the first Black woman to be ordained as an Episcopal priest.

A vision of what could be is what inspires us to start on a journey. Sometimes we move decisively toward a goal; other times we begin only with a subtle movement. In either case, the road is long and there are no shortcuts. We begin by taking the first step, and every step that follows. Along the way we are changed, the goal itself may change, or perhaps it may not even be realized. But in deciding to start, we put ourselves on the path of our transformation. The vision may be audacious, but along with it comes a sense of excitement and purpose. In the inevitable moments of disappointment and failure, we learn to be brave and not give up.

Deciding to start on a courageous journey has the effect of weaving our past experiences into a larger tapestry of meaning. Nothing is lost or wasted. We recognize that our efforts are beholden to those who went before us. From their perspective, our decision to start may, in fact, be a continuation of the work that they began, or the realization in our lifetimes of what they could only imagine in their dreams. When we decide to start toward something that requires courage, we are often creating new possibilities for those who come after us. Our example may be the one to inspire others to turn toward their Jerusalem, whatever the path God has set before them.

There are, however, no guarantees when we start that we will reach the shore beckoning on our horizon. There are forces in life and in our world that stall and prevent forward movement, failures from which we cannot recover, and circumstances beyond our control and beyond our power to change that call for a different order of courage, its own new start.

CHAPTER FOUR

Accepting What You Do Not Choose

God, grant me the serenity to accept the
things I cannot change,
the courage to change the things I can,
and the wisdom to know the difference.

—Reinhold Niebuhr[1]

The news didn't come as a complete surprise. My sister had known for months that something wasn't right. But when Christine called early on a January morning to tell me that her life partner, Jack, had been diagnosed with stage IV lung cancer, there was shock, nonetheless, and dread in her voice.

Jack's prognosis wasn't good, but his doctors encouraged him to remain hopeful and he immediately began a chemotherapy regimen. The side effects were awful. Christine's life, once filled with her grandchildren's activities, volunteer work, and helping out at Jack's business, was now entirely oriented toward his care. She commuted most days to the hospital for his treatments or to keep him company when he was too sick to come home. Those mornings, we often called each other from our cars.

One day Christine told me that she now knew every corner of the hospital complex, from the lower levels of the parking garage, through the labyrinthine hallways, and onto numerous floors. "It wasn't in my plan for 2019," she said, laughing wryly, "but I guess this is what God wanted me to learn."

I knew Christine didn't really believe that God had orchestrated Jack's illness so she might acquire this mundane bit of information. It was her way of expressing how she was coming to terms with an awful situation, trusting that God was somewhere in the mess of it all. I had always admired my sister for her strength and do-what-has-to-be-done approach to life; now I watched in awe as she cared for Jack with determined love.

They enjoyed a brief respite after his last round of chemotherapy, when Jack was declared cancer free. But with the good news came his doctor's sober advice that now was the time for him to get his affairs in order and do everything on his bucket list. Christine went into high gear. She encouraged Jack's brothers to take him on a Gulf Coast fishing expedition, his great passion. She ensured that he spent time with his children and grandchildren, and she finalized the transfer of his business to one of his daughters. That summer, they visited Yellowstone National Park, a dream vacation clouded by Jack's growing fatigue.

When they returned from Yellowstone, the doctors confirmed that the tumors had returned and spread. Jack's options were diminishing, yet he remained determined to fight, and Christine quietly supported him. In conversations with me, however, she expressed sadness at how he was choosing to spend his last days. She had to hold back her anger at his doctors. Why were they giving him false hope?

Paul and I flew to Texas in late July. Jack, a shadow of his former self, greeted us warmly. Christine looked exhausted, yet without complaint she took him each day for radiation, after which he would sleep. In the late afternoons, we sat on the back porch as he smoked. I asked if he was afraid. "It doesn't look good," he acknowledged, but said no more. When the time came to say goodbye, Jack thanked us for coming. "I look forward to seeing you again," he said. On the day we returned home, his doctors told Jack there was nothing more they could do. Before Christine had time to set up the hospital bed she had ordered, he was gone.

There was nothing in this situation that Christine would have chosen for herself, and certainly not for Jack. Watching her navigate his illness and care, I was reminded of Howard Thurman's words about the spiritual strength required to accept an unchosen fate as one's destiny, and the grace that comes from that acceptance. Among the many things Christine had to make peace with was Jack's inability to accept what he could not change, and a health-care system unwilling to let him die in peace. The only thing within her control was how she would respond. She chose love.

Accepting what we did not choose and cannot change is one of the most courageous decisions we make, and the most difficult. When faced with a terrible situation, denial is often our first response as our brains struggle to take in an unwanted new reality. When the facts stubbornly persist, we do whatever we can to avert the outcome we most dread. This is instinctual, for we were created for life. Even the Serenity Prayer, with its emphasis on accepting the things we cannot change, also exhorts us to change the things we can. But we generally don't get to acceptance until we've exhausted all other options.

Acceptance can look like passivity or resignation, but it's not. For in acceptance, we actively engage with whatever we're faced with, precisely because *this is what we're faced with*. There's no turning away and no turning back. I once experienced severe air turbulence, the kind that made us all wonder if the airplane was going down. When the captain came over the loudspeaker during the worst of it, he conveyed both gravity and calmness: "Folks, as you can tell, we've hit a rough patch. I'm sorry to say that there's no getting around it—so hold on tight. The only way out of this one is through."

As someone who rises nearly every Sunday morning to speak of God, I've learned that one of the most important functions of preaching is to name reality as best I can. That task was especially clear to me on March 8, 2020, when I spoke from the Canterbury pulpit of Washington National Cathedral after we had abruptly closed all Episcopal churches in the Diocese of Washington. This was in the early days of the COVID-19 pandemic, when closing our churches felt like the most drastic decision I would ever make as bishop. Little did we know how many more dramatic decisions would follow as the pandemic came to dominate our lives. We were all hoping for a quick end.

I realized that my task was to say what no one, myself included, wanted to hear: it was time to brace ourselves for a long stretch of hardship and uncertainty. The refrain from an old hymn kept running through my mind: "Grant us wisdom, grant us courage, for the facing of this hour."[2] I thought of all who had spoken from that same pulpit during other seasons of national calamity—wars, terrorist attacks, natural disasters—and how few crises end as quickly as we first hope. Then I remembered young Frodo Baggins, the reluctant hero of J. R. R. Tolkien's *The Lord of the Rings*, and his acceptance of a fate he did not want.

In Tolkien's fictional land of wizards, elves, and gentle creatures known as hobbits, evil looms on the horizon. A dark lord named Sauron seeks to dominate and enslave all inhabitants of Middle-earth. The power he needs is contained in a magic ring that has been lost for centuries, until an old hobbit named Bilbo finds it and gives it to his nephew, Frodo. The wise wizard Gandalf knows both the history of the ring and the necessity of preventing it from falling into Sauron's hands. He believes that Frodo is the one destined to carry the ring to the one place it can be destroyed, a fiery volcano known as Mordor.

In an exchange that has inspired readers for generations, Gandalf exhorts Frodo to have courage. "The ring came to you for a reason," Gandalf tells him. "There is comfort in that." "I wish the ring had never come to me," Frodo despairs. "I wish this had never happened." "So do all who live in such times," Gandalf replies. "But while we cannot choose the times we live in, we can choose how to respond to the time we are given." Frodo says at last, "I will take the ring, but I do not know the way." Gandalf later assures him, "There are other forces at work in this world, Frodo, besides the will of evil."[3]

I recounted that exchange from the pulpit that day, allowing Frodo to give voice to our collective wish that the pandemic had never happened. Yet in our time it came—not the first pandemic, nor the last. The story our children and grandchildren will want us to tell someday is not *that* we lived through the COVID pandemic, but *how* we did and what we learned. I wanted to convey that most audacious of faith statements: there are forces for good at work in the world, even in the darkest hours. We are our best selves, I said, when we join those forces and do our part, tipping the scales ever more slightly toward the good.

I had no idea how long the pandemic would endure, how many lives would be lost, and how each variant would cause another wave of infections, illness, and death. As we made our way through 2020, COVID-19 laid bare the fault lines of our society, including racial and socioeconomic inequities, a weak public healthcare system, and political polarization. As disproportionate death rates among people of color and instances of police and vigilante violence against Black Americans dominated the news, some began to speak of two interrelated pandemics: the coronavirus and systemic racism.

Two years into the pandemic, after the summer of protests sparked by the police murder of George Floyd, the tumultuous presidential election of 2020, and the violent insurrection at the U.S. Capitol, I was invited to lead a seminar on leadership for an ecumenical group of clergy. I was glad to accept, for I knew that I would be among fellow practitioners who were expecting me to be a learner alongside learners, not an expert. We were all making our way through the terrain of what the Harvard Business School professors Ronald Heifetz and Marty Linksy defined as "adaptive work," the challenges leaders face when their communities and organizations can no longer rely on what served them well in the past, but rather must make an evolutionary leap in order to thrive in a new environment.[4]

Near the end of a day of lively conversation, one of the seminar faculty, a man I've admired for nearly thirty years, asked how I would respond to several of his colleagues who were wondering if the time had come to leave this country, for fear of the direction it was taking. I had the sense that he may have been asking for himself, a Jewish man raised in the shadow of the Holocaust, as well as for others. Choosing my words carefully, I replied, "In crucible moments, everyone must make difficult decisions. Sometimes the wisest, most life-affirming decision is to leave because personal safety is not a given, nor is justice assured in our criminal justice system. But this country needs leaders now, and citizens who can face things as they are, work to change what can be changed, and not give up hope for the future." I repeated something I had said in October 2021 to colleagues in our diocese as we spoke of the future of our denomination: "If this ship is going down, I'm going down with it—but not without doing everything I can to keep that from happening."

As I spoke, Dietrich Bonhoeffer, the German pastor and theologian who lived during the rise of Adolf Hitler, came to mind. Although most German Christian leaders in the 1930s and early '40s aligned themselves with a pro-Nazi German Christian movement (Deutsche Evangelische Kirche), Bonhoeffer joined a resistance group known as the Confessing Church (Bekennende Kirche). When Bonhoeffer traveled to Great Britain and the United States to seek support from Christian leaders among the Allied nations, his friends and colleagues urged him to remain in exile, yet he chose to return to Germany. In a letter to Reinhold Niebuhr, who before the war had invited Bonhoeffer to teach at Union Theological Seminary in New York, he explained why: "I will have no right to participate in the reconstruction of Christian life in Germany after the war if I do not share in the trials of this time with my people."[5]

Bonhoeffer knew that his decision put his life in danger, and indeed he was arrested in 1943 and executed by the Gestapo on April 9, 1945. "No one person is responsible for all the world's injustice and suffering," Bonhoeffer wrote from prison in 1943. "Still we must take part in Christ's greatness of heart, in the responsible action that in freedom lays hold of the hour. . . . What remains is on the very narrow path, sometimes barely discernible, of taking each day as if it were the last and yet living it faithfully and responsibly as if there were yet again to be a great future."[6]

"As much as any of us might want to walk away," I told my colleagues over Zoom that day, "this is our time. We did not choose the circumstances in which we find ourselves. All we can do is decide how we will respond."

Accepting what we do not choose invariably means making peace with suffering, a theme that runs through both the Jewish and

Christian texts of the Bible. For the apostle Paul, author of most of the letters in the New Testament, suffering was a means of solidarity with Christ, whose message he had originally rejected. A Jewish leader in his own right, Paul never knew Jesus of Nazareth, and prior to his conversion experience, he took it upon himself to persecute Jesus' followers in an effort to eradicate what he considered a dangerous sect. But after his spiritual encounter with the Resurrected Christ and a period of self-imposed isolation, Paul emerged as a tireless evangelist and community organizer who almost single-handedly spread Jesus' message throughout the Roman Empire.

Paul believed that suffering was necessary for spiritual maturity and mystical union with Christ. In his letter to the Romans, he goes so far as to say that followers of Jesus should boast in their suffering,

> *knowing that suffering produces endurance, and endurance produces character, and character produces hope, and hope does not disappoint us, because God's love has been poured into our hearts through the Holy Spirit that has been given to us.*[7]

Paul wasn't masochistic, but he was persuaded that God's love for humankind found its fullest expression in Jesus' crucifixion. As a follower of a crucified Lord, he felt called to take his share of suffering for love's sake.

Paul didn't dwell on the hardships he endured for his efforts to make Christ known. Writing from a Roman prison cell to a Christian community he had established in Philippi (in modern-day Greece), Paul assured his worried friends that he was at peace: "I

want to know Christ and the power of his resurrection and the sharing of his sufferings by becoming like him in his death."[8] In another
letter attributed to Paul, he wrote, "I am now rejoicing in my
sufferings for your sake, and in my flesh I am completing what is
lacking in Christ's afflictions for the sake of the body, that is, the
church."[9]

Only once did Paul give a glimpse into his inner struggle, and
how he came to accept what he did not choose. In his second letter to
the Christians in Corinth, Paul referred to a "thorn in the flesh" that
he believed was given to him "to keep him from being too elated":

> Three times I appealed to the Lord about this, that it would leave
> me, but he said to me, "My grace is sufficient for you, for power is
> made perfect in weakness." So, I will boast all the more gladly of
> my weaknesses, so that the power of Christ may dwell in me.
> Therefore I am content with weaknesses, insults, hardships, per-
> secutions, and calamities for the sake of Christ; for whenever I
> am weak, then I am strong.[10]

Paul does not disclose the nature or source of his pain, only that
it was always with him. His prayer that he be spared his suffering
was answered, not in its release, but by the grace that allowed him
to find meaning in it.

Paul's example is one that I often turn to, although I confess to
praying far more than three times for the things I did not choose to
be taken from me. Yet when those prayers go unanswered, or the
answer, as in Paul's case, is no, where else is there to turn?

Chronic pain is my daily reminder of the challenge and the

grace of learning to live with what I cannot change. It first surfaced as a severe case of tendonitis in one of my ankles that lasted for several months. I had never known such pain before, and I ignored it at first, keeping up my normal routines of physical activity. Before long I could barely walk. Then I was forced to rest my ankle, and inactivity starkly revealed what I had always suspected—that exercise was how I managed to keep depression at bay. Despair washed over me in waves.

When my ankle finally began to improve, the pain migrated to my lower back. Although I could now walk, sitting for any length of time was agony, as was lying down. Months went by with no relief, then a year, and then another. I learned how exhausting chronic pain can be, and how hard it is to talk about. Everyone wanted me to feel better, and I felt like I was letting them down. My physical therapist mother kept saying, "Your back shouldn't hurt," as if that settled the matter. I could still function in my daily life, and over time, those around me assumed that I had healed. I vacillated between avoiding the subject and wishing that people cared more.

In those years, I consulted with all manner of specialists and underwent multiple tests, with no conclusive diagnosis. I saw several chiropractors, each offering relief that never lasted more than a few hours. In desperation, I signed up for ten Rolfing sessions, a treatment known equally for its discomfort and its expense. During my last visit, the Rolfer told me that there wasn't anything wrong with my back. "Your brain is caught in a pain loop," he said with authority. "The only thing you can do is to keep telling yourself that there's nothing wrong. Eventually your brain will get the message." For a while I believed him and tried to retrain my brain, but it didn't work. In fact, nothing "worked" in that I live with chronic back pain to this day.

In time, I found partial relief through a combination of exercise, periodic chiropractic treatment, posture improvement, and meditation. But first I had to accept the fact that the pain wasn't going away. I found another chiropractor who took my suffering seriously, and I saw him weekly for about six months. He showed me an X-ray displaying the curvature of my spine and the slight jutting out of my chin, perhaps caused by some injury I can't remember.

At our last session, he took another X-ray. After studying it carefully, he turned to me. "We've done as much as we can to correct it," he said. My heart sank. "So it's never going to improve?" I asked. "Probably not," he said. "But this may be one of those conditions that paradoxically promotes health." Then he added something that has become a mantra for my life: "If you tend to the weakness of your back, and surround it with strength, you will live a long and healthy life."

His words have proven true. Every morning I wake up with an aching back; every morning I take the necessary time to stretch my muscles until the pain abates. At the end of the day, I stretch again so that I can sleep through the night. I've learned that if I want to live without constant discomfort, these exercises aren't optional, and over the years they have had the auxiliary effect of keeping my body flexible and relatively fit. If the pain becomes too distracting, as it sometimes does, there are a few other remedies to draw upon, but I've long since given up the notion that I will ever be without it. Acceptance is liberating, in that I no longer fight with my body, which allows my brain to focus on other things. Perhaps that was what the Rolfer was trying to tell me. Living with pain also has given me empathy for others who suffer from chronic illness and all the other circumstances we would never choose for ourselves but must learn to accept.

Many people endure pain far greater than mine, without relief and without meaning to be gained from it, and in no way do I mean to minimize their suffering. At the same time, there is a mystery embedded in pain that all major faith traditions point to, and those who have experienced it testify to its transformative power. They do not judge others who do not share their experience, but they want us to know that it's possible to find meaning in adversity, even the circumstances we would have given anything to avoid. The ones who offer a more nuanced, even positive, interpretation of their own pain have given me hope in mine and the assurance of blessing that lies on the other side of acceptance.

Among those who speak and write with the authority of first-hand knowledge is Rachel Naomi Remen, MD, one of the earliest practitioners of integrative medicine, or mind/body health. Now in her eighties, Remen has lived for more than sixty years with Crohn's disease, a chronic, progressive, and at times excruciatingly painful intestinal condition. In her lifetime of experience as both patient and doctor, she has lived with the limitations of Western medicine to cure, alongside our innate capacity for healing. She has listened to and gathered the stories of countless men, women, and children who also found reservoirs of wisdom and peace within their suffering.

In *Kitchen Table Wisdom: Stories That Heal*, Dr. Remen gives testimony to what she has learned by being attentive to her own life and to the lives of her patients. Early in her medical training, she realized that the stories people told her were far more compelling than the diseases she was attempting to treat. "This was the conversation of people in bomb shelters, people under siege, people in times of common crisis everywhere," she writes. "I listened to human beings who were suffering and responding to their suffering in ways as unique as their fingerprints. Their stories were inspiring, moving, and important. In time, the truth in them began to heal me."[11]

Remen describes her own journey to acceptance, and how she came to it in bits and pieces over time. In an essay titled "Damming the River," she describes the anger she felt, at age fifteen, in response to the disease that had suddenly defined her life: "I hated all the well people. I hated the side of my family that had passed me these genes. I hated my body. I was in this state of rage for almost ten years."[12]

A turning point came in medical school when she was offered a residency at a premier training hospital. It was her dream position, but her unyielding fatigue caused her to doubt that she could handle the work. She recounts walking along a body of water, feeling desolate and envious of others her age who had seemingly boundless energy. The familiar anger flooded her senses. "But for some reason, this time I didn't drown in it," she writes. "Instead, I sort of noticed it go by and something inside me said, 'You think you have no vitality? Here's your vitality.'"[13]

Remen realized that her rage was an expression of a deeper force within her, the part of her that loved life and wanted to live to the fullest. Over the years, it had helped her fight against the limitations of her disease. Now she understood that it was time to channel that fierce energy in a new way. "It was like the power of a dammed river," she writes.[14] She chose to lay down her anger, her desire to blame others and find fault in the world, ready at last to accept the pain and embrace the gift of her life.

Remen never encourages her patients to "get past" their anger, for it may be what is keeping them alive. Rather, she listens and waits for each person to discover other expressions of the life force within. Her acceptance of anger in whatever form it presents itself has helped me appreciate its place and power in the healing process, while at the same time consider the full creative range of possibilities within us, so that as we come to terms with what we cannot change, we might also know joy.

Acceptance, unlike avoidance or denial, never looks away from suffering but rather faces it directly and seeks to place it within a larger narrative. Remen writes of a time when, after major abdominal surgery, she developed peritonitis, a life-threatening inflammation of the membrane lining the abdominal wall, along with sepsis, an equally grave condition. She was rushed back for further surgery. When the nurses came to change her bandages the next day, Remen looked down at her body, expecting to see a long incision held together with stitches. Instead, there was a gaping hole, as if she were still in the operating room. Because of her infections, the wound would be left open to heal on its own.

Remen couldn't bring herself to look at her abdomen again. When the nurses came in each day to change the dressings, she turned her head, unable to face what she was certain was a mortal wound. This went on until it dawned on her that, in fact, she wasn't dying. A new thought occurred to her: "*If I was going to live with it, I had to see it,*"[15] she writes. Such is the courage of acceptance—to look directly at what we dread and trust that we can survive. When she did, Remen was astounded to see that the wound had begun to heal.

Yet not every wound heals and there are illnesses with which we cannot live for long. Remen is no stranger to the limitations of the human body. In those instances, she stresses the importance of allowing grief to surface. Rising from that grief, she assures us, new possibilities emerge, and when cures are not possible, there can be healing of a different order. This isn't an answer we can hear when we are still holding on to a hope for recovery. Yet when that hope is gone, some among us attest to feeling alive in a new way. In a collection of essays titled *My Grandfather's Blessings: Stories of Strength, Refuge, and Belonging,* Remen writes, "As a physician, I have accompanied people as they have discovered in themselves an unexpected strength, a courage beyond what they thought would have been possible, an unsuspected sense of compassion or a capacity for love deeper than they have ever dreamed."[16] I think that is what Jesus meant when he likened the Kingdom of God within us to a pearl of great price.

In the Christian faith, we see in Jesus the presence of God in human form, accepting the world as it is and revealing to us the nature of divine love. We can take solace from the fact that even Jesus struggled, and at the final hour prayed for deliverance from the pain and suffering of death. Three of the four accounts of Jesus' life make no effort to shield us from the agony that Jesus endured in the hours leading to his crucifixion.

According to three of the four Gospels—Mark, Matthew, and Luke—on the night before his death, Jesus shares a Passover meal with his twelve disciples and then retreats to a garden to pray. His closest disciples follow him there, but as the night wears on, sleep overtakes them, and Jesus is essentially alone. He prays these heart-breaking words: "Father, if it be possible, let this cup pass from me; yet not what I want, but what you want."[17]

For all the clarity he once felt about his vocation and the initial acceptance of his fate, on that last night, Jesus prays to God that he be spared. This poignant scene assures us of his full humanity—that he, too, knew fear and the desire to live. We aren't told how long Jesus struggled between his appeal to God and coming to re-newed acceptance of what lay ahead. We only know that at some point during that long, lonely night, Jesus embraced his fate and made it an offering of sacrificial love.

Throughout his life and most especially in death, God revealed in Jesus the power of what Dr. Martin Luther King Jr. called "re-demptive suffering," a mystical, and admittedly controversial, asser-tion that undeserved suffering has spiritual power beyond our understanding or experience. For Christians, the crucified Jesus would become an icon of all human suffering, and his resurrection an eternal promise that pain and death will not have the final word.

The notion that suffering can wrest good from evil finds rich expression in biblical literature. Particularly influential for the early Christian interpretation of Jesus' death are a series of poetic pas-sages from the Jewish prophetic writings known as the "Songs of the

Suffering Servant." Found in the Book of Isaiah, the poems are attributed to an anonymous author referred to as Second Isaiah because of their distinct voice and historical context. They describe a person of gentle spirit who was despised for his goodness. God chooses this servant for a mission of reconciliation and healing: "I am the Lord, I have called you in righteousness, I have taken you by the hand and kept you; I have given you as a covenant to the people, a light to the nations, to open the eyes that are blind, to bring out the prisoners from the dungeon, from the prison those who sit in darkness."[18]

The most explicit expression of the servant's call to suffer is found in Isaiah, chapter 53, told from the perspective of those who benefit from the pain the servant has endured:

> Surely he has borne our infirmities
> and carried our diseases;
> yet we accounted him stricken,
> struck down by God, and afflicted.
> But he was wounded for our transgressions,
> crushed for our iniquities;
> upon him was the punishment that made us whole,
> and by his bruises we are healed.[19]

In Judaism, the Suffering Servant is understood as the nation of Israel, called to embrace the trials of exile and discover in the collective pain of its people a path of redemption for all nations. For early Christians, the Suffering Servant became the interpretative lens through which to grasp the meaning of Jesus' death on a cross.

Our spiritual forebears struggled, as we do today, with the question that has no satisfactory answer: *why* must we suffer? Efforts to explain why the Servant had to suffer and Jesus had to die an agonizing death abound in the biblical texts. As with our own attempts to find answers for our pain, the reasoning can be unsettling and even offensive. At one point, Second Isaiah suggests that God has intentionally hurt the Servant:

> *Yet it was the will of the Lord to crush him with pain. . . .*
> *The righteous one, my servant, shall make many righteous,*
> *and he shall bear their iniquities.*[20]

It is a troubling view of God, held in constant tension in biblical texts and contemporary interpretations, with images of God as full of mercy and loving-kindness.

Early Christians saw in Jesus' death a similar fulfillment of God's will. Jesus himself came to that conclusion in his final hours, and throughout the New Testament there are many references to Jesus dying "for our sins." As the apostle Paul writes in his Letter to the Romans, "since all have sinned and fall short of the glory of God; they are now justified by his grace as a gift, through the redemption that is in Christ Jesus, whom God put forward as a sacrifice of atonement by his blood, effective through faith."[21]

Thus emerged from these searing faith experiences of the nation of Israel and the earliest followers of Jesus a theological assertion of sacrifice, rooted in the premise that God's righteousness has no choice but to demand recompense for the sins of humankind. What makes this otherwise appallingly cruel view of God somewhat palatable is that in Jesus, God *is* the atoning sacrifice. In this light, Jesus' sacrifice becomes an expression of how far God will go in love for us.

I have struggled with this view of God and of Jesus' mission for most of my life of faith, and I am not alone. For Christians and non-Christians alike, this view of Jesus' suffering is the most challenging and, frankly, unappealing, aspects of our tradition. It doesn't answer to any real satisfaction why the innocent suffer, for its focus is on restitution for human sin, which, in the biblical worldview, is an affront to God. While I recognize my personal need for a saving grace that is greater than my sinfulness and believe that Jesus died for the sins of the world, nonetheless, for me atonement theory remains at best an incomplete understanding of Jesus' redemptive suffering. It suggests that his death was transactional, something between God and Jesus alone, and the most important thing to know about Jesus. But in the words of the late Rachel Held Evans, "Jesus did not simply die to save us from our sins; Jesus *lived* to save us from our sins. His life and teachings show us the way to liberation."[22] Jesus approached his death trusting in God's love despite what he had to endure. The earliest Christians knew beyond a shadow of a doubt that Jesus' way was one of sacrificial love.

Seen through the lens of love, the Servant's suffering and Christ's death provide a window into God's heart. It is in Jesus' entire life, culminating in his death on the cross, that we see the one in whom "the fullness of God was pleased to dwell."[23] Or, as written in the Gospel of John, Jesus is an expression of God's light that "shines in the darkness, and the darkness did not overcome it."[24] In Jesus, we see the human face of God, as one who suffers alongside humankind to reveal the depth of divine love. Those called to follow him are to walk on that same path of love, taking up our own cross as life demands.

Admittedly, when faced with trauma and suffering, there are no answers that satisfy, and well-meaning platitudes can feel like salt in the wound. As Kate Bowler writes in her memoir about life after a stage IV cancer diagnosis, *Everything Happens for a Reason and Other Lies I've Loved,* we don't realize how empty those words are until we're on the receiving end of someone's attempt to make sense of our tragedy: "Apparently God is busy going around closing doors and opening windows," she wryly observes. "He can't get enough of that."[25] Worse still are theological assertions that suffering is somehow our fault.

Without question, the most helpful responses to suffering are empathic presence and efforts to ameliorate the pain and prevent its recurrence. Yet when those efforts fail, we are left to find whatever meaning we can in the trials we endure. In Jesus and in the Suffering Servant before him, we have examples of what it looks like to face suffering for what it is and, by grace, find within it a path of personal and societal transformation. We would never choose this path or wish it on those we love. But when there is no way out, it's at least comforting, and at times emboldening, to know that those who have walked the path before us were able to speak of it with humility and a gratitude that we cannot understand until we find ourselves in the same place.

I was eight years old when the Reverend Dr. Martin Luther King Jr. was assassinated, and it wasn't until college that I first encountered him through his writings and recorded speeches. I spent hours in the library reading and listening to his words, mesmerized. This was during the Central American wars, and I was in awe of religious leaders dying alongside indigenous farmers and university students in the struggles for justice. Yet here was a Christian leader who inspired social change through nonviolent means in my own country and gave expression to our shared faith with a brilliance unlike anyone I had ever encountered. King embodied redemptive suffering—the acceptance of what one would never choose for the sake of love and a greater good—until his untimely and tragic death at age thirty-nine.

King did not appear on the American religious and political landscape in a vacuum, nor was he singularly responsible, as the media still often portrays him, for the accomplishments of the Civil Rights Movement. Yet unlike any of his contemporaries, King captured the imagination of those who dared to believe that the time had come at last for our nation to reckon with slavery's legacy and the evils of racism. As labor historian Michael K. Honey writes in *Going Down Jericho Road: The Memphis Strike, Martin Luther King's Last Campaign*, "King's religious framework, his stunning eloquence, his learning, his ability to place his demands within the framework of the Constitution and the American creed of freedom—all made him a powerful spokesperson, and the mass media gave King phenomenal attention."[26] His writings and recorded speeches remain a boundless source of political analysis and spiritual insight.

The well of King's convictions ran deep. In *The Power of Unearned Suffering: The Roots and Implications of Martin Luther King, Jr.'s Theodicy*,

Mika Edmondson traces his lineage as the child and grandchild of Baptist preachers, formed by the long legacy of his enslaved and oppressed forbears struggling to make sense of their suffering:

> *Beneath the sweltering sun of southern cotton fields, they shouldered on with the hope that the omnipotent God could "make a way out of no way"—that because of Christ, God would somehow bring good from the evils inflicted on them. . . . This hope in God's redemptive purposes in suffering has sustained black Christians through the historic brutalities like chattel slavery, Jim Crow, the lynching tree, and segregation.*[27]

As a child, King's parents had instilled in him both a strong aversion to segregation and a belief that there were divine purposes at work in the struggle for freedom. He studied sociology at Morehouse College, then theology at Crozer Theological Seminary and Boston University, where he earned his doctorate at the age of twenty-five. Like his professors and mentors, including Howard Thurman, he was inspired by Mahatma Gandhi's compelling example of nonviolence. He came to believe, as he wrote in 1957, "the Negro may be God's appeal to this age."[28]

There is a poignantly hopeful tone in his early writings. Fresh from the triumph of the Montgomery Bus Boycotts in 1956, King wrote: "The Negro people of Montgomery, exhausted by the humiliating experiences that they had constantly faced on the buses, expressed in a massive act of noncooperation their determination to be free. They came to see that it was ultimately more honorable to walk the streets in dignity than to ride the buses in humiliation."[29] He drew a clear distinction between passive suffering that only perpetuated injustice and suffering freely chosen as destiny that was rich with redemptive possibilities. Like Gandhi, King called his people to absorb the blows of violent reaction to their peaceful demands for equal treatment under the law as a means of social transformation that, for a time, seemed close at hand.

King's early optimism was matched by his own capacity and willingness to endure hardship, something he rarely wrote about or spoke of publicly. One exception came at the specific request of the editors of *The Christian Century*, when in a brief addendum to an article published in 1960, he acknowledged the personal cost to him and his family: "Due to my involvement in the struggle for the freedom of my people, I have known very few quiet days," he wrote in striking understatement, and then matter-of-factly listed some of what he had endured: five arrests and time spent in Alabama jails, two bombings of his home, multiple death threats, and a stabbing that almost killed him. More than once, he admitted, the burdens felt too heavy to carry and he considered retreating to a quieter life. "But each time such a temptation appeared," he wrote, "something came to strengthen and sustain my determination. I have learned now that the Master's burden is light precisely when we take his yoke upon us."[30]

King also shared what this journey of inner transformation had been like for him: "As my sufferings mounted, I soon realized there were two ways I could respond to my situation: either to react with bitterness or seek to transform the suffering into a creative force. I decided to follow the latter course. Recognizing the necessity for suffering I have tried to make of it a virtue."[31] Redemptive suffering was not merely a political strategy for King; it was a way of life.

The early gains of the Civil Rights Movement had always been for King the first step in addressing the greatest of social inequities: poverty and lack of access to education, employment, and safe living conditions. But when he turned his attention to economic issues, many of his admirers seemed genuinely surprised, and these later writings still receive less attention and acclaim than his entreaties for racial equity. Indeed, every choice King made in the final years of his life sparked controversy: the decision to move to Chicago to highlight the perniciousness of racism in the North, his growing focus on issues of poverty and economic discrimination; and, most dramatically, his public opposition to the Vietnam War.

Although long reviled by white supremacists and anticommunists, King now fell out of favor among many white liberals and the once-adoring press. After his anti-war statements, many former allies, most notably President Lyndon Johnson, severed all ties. Crowds still flocked to hear him whenever he spoke, which gave him a national platform. Yet his continued prominence mobilized his detractors, including J. Edgar Hoover, the director of the Federal Bureau of Investigation, who was intent on destroying King. There was also increasing conflict within his inner circle of advisers as they struggled to operationalize his vision of a multiracial movement of poor people to descend upon Washington, D.C.

If King had known few quiet days in 1960, by 1967, his life was in a frenzy. The Poor People's Campaign was his last plea for nonviolence in a country that seemed to be spinning out of control. He was consumed with a vision to unite the working poor of all races in a common demand for the restructuring of the United States economy. It was poverty, he believed, that destroyed lives and fueled the racism, despair, and violence that plagued our land. If the strategy failed, he soberly told a reporter in 1967, all he could do is "say to the nation, 'I've done my best.'"[32] Although in public he remained resolute, privately he struggled with depression, fatigue, and doubt. He began to make plans for his succession, all the while pouring everything he had into what his closest allies feared was a doomed effort.

While attending a ministers' conference in February 1968, King heard about the sanitation workers' strike in Memphis. Another attendee, Pastor Billy Kyles, described how, in a spontaneous act of collective defiance, Black workers rose to protest life-threatening conditions and starvation wages. The city government refused to negotiate, and as garbage piled up in the city streets, the populace divided along racial lines. Kyles was the first to suggest that King come to Memphis, but his staff quickly responded that he was too busy organizing the Poor People's Campaign to make the trip.[33]

As the Memphis strike dragged on, support in the Black community began to wane. City officials remained intransigent, and the police became more brazen in their violence. The workers remained committed to nonviolent protest, but others advocated a more confrontational approach. With greater urgency now, several local ministers urged King to come, persuaded that only he could unify a rapidly fragmenting movement. This time, he did not hesitate in saying yes, against the unanimous counsel of his staff. It would be yet another burden on his already-crushing schedule, but by now, King's acceptance of personal suffering had become muscle memory.

Thousands turned out to hear King speak on what would be the first of three visits to Memphis in the last days of his life. The energy and sense of unity of the crowd buoyed his spirits. He saw in the sanitation workers' courage and solidarity what he wanted to invoke across the nation—a movement of working people standing with dignity to demand safe conditions and a living wage. He encouraged the strikers to persevere and urged the Black community to stay away from work and school to pressure the mayor to come to the negotiation table. It was the first time King had ever proposed a general strike, yet it was in line with what he was increasingly persuaded would be necessary across the nation.

After King finished speaking that day, Joseph Rosenbloom writes, "As though seized by a sudden force, he returned to the rostrum. In a strong, vibrant voice he proclaimed that Memphis could mark 'the beginning of the Washington movement' and announced that he would soon return to march with the strikers and their supporters."[34] King's fate and that of the Poor People's Campaign was now bound to the conflict in Memphis.

The one-day work stoppage on March 28 was a complete disaster. Strikers and supporters had gathered early waiting for King to lead them, but his plane was late and the march had to start without him. When he finally arrived, chaos ensued as hundreds swarmed around him. Exhausted from days of nonstop travel, King was disoriented and unprepared for the crowd's response to his presence. Fearing he would be trampled, his security team quickly ushered him to safety.[35] Meanwhile, violence broke out throughout the city.

Protestors threw bottles and rocks, looted shops, and torched cars. Police responded with indiscriminate violence, sending panic through the crowds of peaceful protestors, wounding scores, arresting hundreds, and killing a sixteen-year-old boy. The violence lasted into the night. Sequestered in a hotel room, King watched television coverage of his worst nightmare in despair.

King left Memphis the next morning visibly shaken, and he spent several days pondering what to do next. Those closest to him worried about his depression and fatigue. But he emerged from his isolation with new resolve, and he announced to his team that they all needed to return to Memphis.[36] The riot had dealt a serious blow to the credibility of their movement, he told them, that if not redeemed, would haunt all their efforts going forward. This time they would stay for five days, work to bring younger Black leaders into the fold, marshal the clergy and unions, and transform the failures of March 28 with a peaceful rally and work stoppage on April 8. The others strongly pushed back on King's proposal at first, but King was adamant, speaking to them with a forcefulness and uncharacteristic anger at their infighting that caught their attention. King's close confidant Andrew Young later wrote of that moment, "As somberly and seriously as we had ever done anything, we decided we would support Martin in any way he needed us."[37] The odds were clearly against them. But as King said on April 3, "Either the Movement lives or dies in Memphis."[38]

The next day, it was King who died.

King almost didn't give the last speech of his life. After a day of travel that began with a bomb threat on his plane and nonstop meetings in Memphis, he was exhausted and ill. A coming storm would surely keep people from the prayer service and rally that evening, he thought. At the last minute he asked his close friend and colleague Ralph Abernathy to address the gathering in his place while he stayed at the hotel to rest. When Abernathy arrived solo, however, the crowd's dismay convinced him to summon King. Reluctantly, King set out amid a driving rainstorm, and when he arrived, he rose to the podium and spoke for nearly an hour. It was, as historian Taylor Branch notes, an elegant weaving together of several of his frequent speech themes in service to the urgency of that moment.[39] The crowd hung on every word.

King told those with ears to hear that he knew that his death was imminent. He began by imagining aloud what he would say if God gave him the opportunity to choose another century in which to live. His response to God was that he would, in fact, choose the present moment. It was a strange thing to consider at a time of so much suffering, he said, "But I know somehow that only when it is dark enough can you see the stars."[40] He acknowledged the threats he received each day and the uncertainty of what lay ahead. "Like anybody, I would like to live a long life," he added. "Longevity has its place. But I'm not concerned about that now. I just want to do God's will." Like Moses before him, God had brought King to the mountaintop to see the Promised Land. "I may not get there with you," he said. "But I want you to know tonight that we, as a people, will get to the promised land! And I'm happy tonight! I'm not fearing *any* man! Mine eyes have seen the *glory* of the coming of the Lord!"[41] His final prediction was one of acceptance, even transcendence, of death.

The sense of destiny that King's parents instilled in him and the

conviction that he lived at a threshold moment of social transformation sustained him to the end, even when it became obvious that he
would not live to see the dream God had placed in his heart. Although often discouraged, King refused to succumb to violence or
give up hope. He accepted what he could not change, and thrust all
his effort into changing what he could.

What never fails to move me is King's compassion. Preaching at
Washington National Cathedral on the last Sunday of his life, he
spoke of the wrenching poverty across our nation, from the northern ghettos to the rural South. He described seeing hundreds of
Black children in Marks, Mississippi, walking the streets barefoot,
and families living with rats and roaches in their deteriorating
apartments. He confessed that he often found himself crying.[42] And
on the stormy night before his assassination, as a way to explain why
he had come back to Memphis, King reflected on Jesus' parable of
the Good Samaritan. In that timeless story, he reminded his listen-
ers, two religious leaders saw a man mortally wounded and chose
to pass him by. Only a man of a despised race, the Samaritan,
stopped to help. That man illustrated what King called a "dangerous unselfishness," which is the essence of love.

> *"The first question the Levite and the priest asked when they*
> *saw the wounded man was 'If I stop to help this man, what will*
> *happen to me?' The Good Samaritan reversed the question. 'If I*
> *do not stop to help this man, what will happen to him?' . . . That*
> *is the question before you tonight. Not, 'If I stop to help the sani-*
> *tation workers, what will happen to me?' But 'If I do not stop to*

help the sanitation workers, what will happen to them?' *That's*
the question."[43]

King's question is at the heart of sacrificial love and acceptance. Compassion for another places us in service to something beyond ourselves and helps us become larger inside than the suffering we must endure or choose to endure. King believed that only love had the power to break the cycles of violence and hate, as revealed by Jesus on the cross. "King saw the cross," writes James Cone in *The Cross and the Lynching Tree*, "as a source of strength and courage, the ultimate expression of God's love for humanity. Unlike others, he never wavered in his commitment to the way of love."[44] The rare shining examples of people like Martin Luther King Jr., who choose acceptance and redemptive suffering, help us believe that such love is both possible and worthy of our best efforts.

Among the many inspired by King whose witness we see in our lifetime is the Most Reverend Michael Curry, presiding bishop of the Episcopal Church. Bishop Curry has dedicated his life in service to Jesus and his way of love. Given a global platform for his message at the British Royal wedding of Prince Harry and Meghan Markle in 2018, he launched an international conversation about the power of redemptive love.

In his most recent book, *Love Is the Way*, he restates King's core conviction as his own: that only unselfish, sacrificial love has the power to heal us and change our world for the better. Only love, he insists, is able to transform us from the people we are into the people God created us to be and transform this world from the nightmare it often is into the dream God has for all his children. The wide appeal of Bishop Curry's message suggests that deep down we all know this truth. Acceptance of the world's suffering as our collective responsibility and responding with sacrificial love is our most authentic task. As individuals and as a species, we must rise to it.

In his book, Curry cites multiple examples of people who chose love as their response to seemingly hopeless situations—from the church elders who cared for him after his mother died when he was twelve to public figures like civil rights activist Fannie Lou Hamer and Franklin Roosevelt's Secretary of Labor Francis Perkins, who fought for justice all their lives. But before they could respond in love, each had to face and accept their pain, not as an expression of God's will, but as the arena in which they were called to embody God's love for someone else. "Love is not always easy," Curry writes, "but like with muscles we get stronger both with repetition and as the burden gets heavier. And it works."[45]

What Curry means by "and it works" isn't that we always get what we want or hope for, but rather that love is God's way. When we choose love in response to what we wish we could change but can't; when we choose love as our response to the world as it is, not as what we wish it were; when we choose love over denial, or anger, or cynicism and withdrawal, we share in God's redeeming of our world. It doesn't make the work any easier, but it gives our efforts a sense of purpose that can carry us through. Through our imperfect efforts, God's grace shines through us in ways we may never know or fully understand.

Acceptance remains among the hardest things asked of us. The price is always high, but in the face of what we would never choose and cannot change, it provides a way forward. We needn't worry if we don't always get it right. In our willingness to stay engaged, God knows that we're all in. Our capacity to love will grow, and through us, God will work quiet miracles that keep hope alive, even in troubling times.

Our lives are full of unforeseen choices, struggles, and callings. Sometimes we can overcome these obstacles, and sometimes we must make peace with them. Sometimes, like Jesus, we are called into the wilderness or to the cross—to physically and spiritually go to those places that challenge us, test us, break us open, and cause something to die within us. Accepting what we did not choose involves a leap of faith that God is present and at work in ways that we cannot comprehend. Sometimes we feel that presence; oftentimes we don't. This kind of acceptance is not passive or fatalistic, but rather a courageous choice at a decisive moment to embrace the places we are broken as an integral part of a courageous life.

CHAPTER FIVE

Stepping Up to the Plate

Who knows? Perhaps you have come to royal
dignity for just such a time as this.

—Esther 4:14

Gregory Boyle is a Jesuit priest and the founder of Homeboy Industries, the largest gang intervention, rehabilitation, and reentry program in the world. This life-changing ministry had its beginnings in Dolores Mission Church, located in the neighborhood with the highest concentration of gang activity in Los Angeles. Boyle served there as parish priest from 1986 to 1992, when young men were both killing and dying at alarming rates. Boyle's first idea was to establish an alternative school for young gang members, and the parish convent where six Belgian nuns lived was the only feasible site. In *Barking to the Choir: The Power of Radical Kinship*, Boyle recounts how he approached them: "'Hey,' I ask, 'Would you guys mind . . . you know . . . moving out . . . and we could turn the convent into a school for gang members?' They looked at me, then at each other, and said simply, '*Sure.*'"[1] The nuns didn't hesitate. With that single word, they did their part.

Like the nuns who said yes, we make some of our most consequential decisions seemingly on the spot, bypassing conscious thought or logical accounting. A situation presents itself, and we respond with something akin to instinct or intuition. Immediacy is the defining characteristic of these moments, although in retrospect, we can sometimes see how long we had been preparing for them. Like a baseball player who has been training for months, there's nothing left to do but step up to the plate and swing. Although baseball is a team sport, stepping up to the plate is the action of one person. Thus it's easy to understand how the phrase became a metaphor to describe those moments when an individual takes the initiative to do what needs to be done.

Stepping up to the plate was an image that came to me during the intense pandemic months of late 2020. COVID-19 infection and deaths were rising at an alarming rate, schools and businesses were closed, and leading up to the presidential election, the mood in the country—and certainly in Washington, D.C.—was fraught. During that time, I received an inordinately high number of requests for assistance. The appeals came from both individuals and organizations. Some of the tasks were relatively small and manageable; others required considerable commitments of time and energy.

That people were reaching out wasn't new. As a minister, it's my job to be helpful. What was different was the quantity of solicitations and their level of intensity; there was an urgency and even desperation in the asking. It occurred to me as I pondered how to respond that my personal fatigue wasn't the most important data point. We were all tired. No matter how I felt, it was time for me to serve wherever and whenever I could.[2] All of my efforts in that season were away from public view, as the majority of "step up to the plate" moments are.

Earlier that year, however, when then-president Trump stood outside the historic St. John's Church holding a Bible, I faced a stepping up moment of greater notoriety than I could ever have anticipated. I had spoken out on matters of equal importance before, including gun violence, immigrant rights, and in protest of the president's racist slurs against the city of Baltimore, all with minimal public reaction apart from the churches I served. This time was different, as if an electric current were running through the country, connecting us all.

When stepping up to the plate in the public arena, it's impossible to know in advance how our actions will be received. There is always the risk of focusing on the response, as if media attention determines the merit or impact of our actions. Yet we know that the most transformative social movements require decades of sustained effort before real change occurs, with many lonely people stepping up long before anyone takes notice. Moreover, public attention, when it comes, is short-lived and seductive, tempting us to stay in the spotlight or seek out the next one, when in the end what matters most is what we do and how we live when no one is watching. That was certainly the case in the summer of 2020.

Immediately after the news of the president's photo op broke, dozens of faith leaders across the region wanted to gather and collectively denounce President Trump's actions and reclaim the sacred space. The energy coming toward our small diocesan staff felt frenetic, but I understood the desire—they wanted to step up, too. We agreed to organize a press conference the next day at St. John's during which we would issue a common condemnation. By Tuesday morning, however, police had blocked off access to the church and demonstrators had spilled over into nearby streets, essentially shutting down that part of the city. On Wednesday, as we attempted to make our way to the podium my staff had hastily set up as close to St. John's as they could get, we were overwhelmed by protestors and dozens of journalists who had staked out their places by the front.

One by one, the religious leaders attempted to speak. Our sound system was terrible, and even standing right next to the podium, I could barely hear what they were saying. Apart from the reporters, no one was paying attention. When it was my turn, I was blinded by the lights in my face, and I couldn't think of a word to say. The spectacle was obviously inconsequential to the demonstrators, many of whom had been physically displaced by the media. Off to the side, I heard a young person say, "Sit down and shut up."

I walked away from the podium and sat down on the street next to him. "We've been in the hot sun all day, and no one has paid us any mind," he said with disgust. "Then you show up, and all the cameras focus on you. When you leave, so will they. But we'll still be here." He was right, of course. I apologized. He shook his head and looked away. A Black minister who was part of the faith leaders gathering came and stood next to me. In a loud voice that conveyed both compassion and authority, he addressed the demonstrators sitting on the street. He thanked them for their witness, encouraged them to persevere, and spontaneously prayed on their behalf. He then took my hand and pulled me to my feet. "Our sister is trying to do what's right," he said. "Please treat her with respect." Most seemed unpersuaded, but one young man turned to me and said, "Don't take it personally. It's been a long, hot day." "More than a day, I imagine," I replied. He nodded. In the realm of justice, and indeed all of life, stepping up to the plate isn't something we do once, but time and again, when it feels as if the world is watching and, more important, when it's not.

Stepping up to the plate is a choice, but there is a dimension to it that feels more like intuition or instinct—we act without relying on conscious thought or even emotion. Sometimes when the moment comes, we instantly know that we have the skills and resources needed for a given task, and we embrace it with confidence. At other times, we feel woefully inadequate and unprepared, yet saying no doesn't feel like an option. In those situations, we learn either to trust a power greater than ourselves acting through our offerings, or the hard but necessary lessons of failure. On still other occasions, we hear a summons that blissfully lifts us out of lesser concerns and preoccupations to do something brave or good, and our past missteps and present foibles don't seem to matter.

Clearly the most ego-affirming version of stepping up to the plate is when we feel well equipped to do it. The task may be large or small. It could be something we're excited about or that we dread, but we can accomplish with relative ease what for others would be more difficult, if not impossible. The stepping up is of disproportionate value to those who benefit from our saying yes. It might be costly in terms of our time and energy expenditure, but the effort rarely leads to burnout. We are functioning from an area of strength.

Years ago, I read about a small group of scientists at the National Institutes of Health who realized that they were on the verge of a breakthrough in treating a rare form of leukemia. Driven by that prospect, they worked around the clock for weeks, missing their children's soccer games and piano recitals so that someone else might live to see their own children play. That's what stepping up to the plate in confidence looks like. Surely that same tenacity helped epidemiologists around the world develop multiple vaccines for COVID-19 in a remarkably short period of time, no doubt at enormous personal sacrifice. Most of us couldn't step up to that particular plate, but they could and did, so that others might live.

In its more dramatic expression, not only are we confident that we *can* do whatever is being asked of us, but we *must*. I again think of Martin Luther King Jr.'s decision to go to Memphis. So, too, for any of us when we feel the pull to show up, or to offer what we have, not necessarily because we want to, but because it's ours to do.

I also am reminded of two occasions in the life of Jesus. The first is from the beginning of his public ministry, as recounted in the Gospel of Luke. Jesus had returned to his hometown of Nazareth after considerable time away. During that time, he had joined the movement of one known as John the Baptist, and at his own baptism, Jesus experienced a profound sense of call. Now he was back home. As was his custom, Jesus went to the synagogue on the Sabbath. When it was his turn to read aloud from the Scriptures, he opened the scroll to the prophet Isaiah:

"The Spirit of the Lord is upon me, because he has anointed me to bring good news to the poor. He has sent me to proclaim release to the captives and recovery of sight to the blind, to let the oppressed go free, to proclaim the year of the Lord's favor."[3]

Jesus rolled up the scroll, sat down, and quietly said, "Today this Scripture has been fulfilled in your hearing."[4] With calm confidence, he identified himself as the one anointed by God. He had heard his own vocation affirmed in Isaiah's words. Jesus was clear, and he was ready. It didn't matter to him when his own community, after initially speaking highly of him, took offense at his words and turned against him. He simply went on his way, to the work that was his to do.

Near the end of his life, Jesus once again stepped up to his destiny, yet with a decidedly different tone and outcome. As recounted in the Gospel of John, religious leaders in Jerusalem had arrested Jesus, ostensibly for healing on the Sabbath. They wanted to silence him for good because his message threatened their hold on the populace and precarious relationship with occupying forces of the Roman government. Lacking the political authority for executions, they appealed to the Roman official Pontius Pilate, suggesting that Jesus was a political risk for the emperor. Dubious of their claims, Pilate had Jesus brought to him. "Are you the King of the Jews?" he asked. Jesus answered, "My kingdom is not from this world. . . . For this I was born, and for this I came into the world, to testify to the truth. Everyone who belongs to the truth listens to my voice." In a question that haunts all who read it, Pilate asked Jesus, "What is truth?" Jesus refused to say anything more, choosing not to plead for his life before the puppet ruler of a despotic empire.[5] He knew that his time had come to die, and he was ready.

———

I once knew a man who faced his own death with a Christ-like degree of acceptance that I pray for the grace to emulate when my time comes. His name was Rod Hardy, and his wife, Katie, was the first office administrator I worked with at St. John's in Minneapolis. When Paul and I moved our young family to Minnesota, Rod and Katie gave us their home for a month while we searched for a place to live. Rod was warm and gregarious, a faithful churchman and devoted father and grandfather. He had everything to live for.

The year I was elected bishop, Rod was diagnosed with cancer. Before long, his doctors told him that there was no effective treatment; at best, he had a few months left. As Paul and I were getting ready to move to Washington, D.C., we stopped by to say goodbye to Katie and Rod, knowing that we would not see Rod alive again. He greeted us warmly from the hospital bed set up in the family room. Before we could ask him how he was feeling, he peppered us with questions, wanting to know all about the new life awaiting us. "I can't wait to hear of all your adventures," he said.

We spoke for perhaps twenty minutes. When Rod began to tire, Paul cleared his throat and told him how much he appreciated his friendship and support over the years. We were all silent for a moment. Then Rod spoke up: "I want people to watch me now, because I'm going to die as if everything we say on Sunday in church is true." He smiled. "Go on. You're going to love your new life." When I returned a few months later for Rod's funeral, Katie told me that he had lived his last days as he said he would, with grace and gratitude.

Even when stepping up to the plate isn't a matter of life and death, it can embolden us to take a leap of faith, stepping into an arena of influence, offering ourselves in service to others. Again, I think of Bishop Michael Curry. Since his election as the presiding bishop of the Episcopal Church in 2015, he has won love and respect across the world. His sermon for the Royal wedding of Prince Harry and Meghan Markle in 2018 inspired the two *billion* people who heard his message of the power of love. "We were made by a power of love, and our lives were meant—and are meant—to be lived in that love. That's why we're here," he said.[6] Addressing the young couple, the family gathered to celebrate that love, and everyone looking on from around the globe, Curry invited us all to imagine a world guided by unselfish, sacrificial love, "where no child will go hungry ever again, poverty will become history, and we will lay down our swords and shields and study war no more."[7] As he spoke, we all wanted that kind of world, *and* to be the kind of people to usher that world into being. That's Bishop Curry's gift.

How he came to be our presiding bishop, with a global platform for his message of love, is another example of stepping up to the plate. For many years, Curry was a beloved leader of the Episcopal Church, serving first as a parish priest and then as bishop of the Diocese of North Carolina. I knew him as a colleague and mentor, and like many, I admired his dynamic preaching, personal warmth, and unwavering commitment to social justice. Throughout his ministry, he was able to take strong public positions on controversial subjects yet maintain genuinely affectionate relationships with those who disagreed.

Early in my years as bishop, Bishop Curry and I were invited by a mutual friend, Bishop Marc Andrus of California, to lead a preaching retreat for clergy. We spent four days together at a lovely conference center in the heart of the Sonoma wine country, speaking on an aspect of ordained ministry all three of us care deeply about. It also gave me the rare opportunity to learn as much as I could from my more seasoned colleagues. One evening I asked Bishop Curry how he managed to do his work with such joy. He said that he tried to focus his energies on the things he did well, which were preaching, teaching, and spending time with clergy. "I don't really like meetings," he told me. "So I try not to accept invitations that involve a lot of sitting around." He seemed truly content.

A few years later, I watched as Bishop Curry stepped with confidence into the election process for presiding bishop. He spoke with grace, good humor, and authority. He was generous and kind to the other candidates. There was not a trace of arrogance in him, only strength and contagious joy. It was as if he knew that he would be elected, the first Black man to lead a predominantly white church with historical ties to slavery and Jim Crow.

I kept thinking back to our conversation in California, because if there was one thing I knew about the role of presiding bishop, it involved attending a lot of meetings and taking on countless administrative burdens—not the work that he told me he loved best. It was clear that personal preference wasn't what motivated Bishop Curry to seek election as presiding bishop, or ambition, for that matter. He simply heard the call. He knew the work ahead would require personal sacrifice, and still he stepped up.

The bishops eligible to vote didn't talk much among ourselves about how we would vote, and there wasn't any explicit campaigning among the four candidates. We held our collective breath as we made our way to the church where the election was to take place. I happened to walk alongside Bishop Curry for a short while, and he took my hand. "For a time such as this, Michael," I said softly, harkening back to the biblical heroine, Esther, at her own iconic stepping up to the plate moment. He stopped, looked directly at me, and said, "Pray for me, my sister. Pray that I never lose sight of Jesus." He knew. And he was ready.

A far more common reaction to the summons to step up, however, lies at the opposite end of the experiential spectrum, when we feel anything *but* ready. These are the times when we know that we can't do what's needed, but we're being asked to do it anyway. Reading the Bible is encouraging here, for there are countless examples throughout both the Jewish and Christian texts of ordinary human beings called by God to do the very thing that feels most impossible.

Some of my favorite biblical characters politely point out to God why they are the wrong person for the job. Moses, for example, insists that he can't possibly be the one to tell the ruler of Egypt to release the Israelites from slavery because he stutters. Jeremiah informs God that no one would listen to him because he is only a boy.

When Isaiah hears God's call, he collapses into shame. "Woe is me," he laments, "I am lost, for I am a man of unclean lips."[8] In each case, God's response is, in effect, "I know who you are. I know your shortcomings. Step up anyway." There is a similar refrain among Jesus' disciples, most notably Simon Peter, whose answer to Jesus' call is, "Go away from me, Lord, for I am a sinful man."[9] But Jesus knows all about Simon Peter, and he is the one Jesus wants by his side.

The message throughout Scripture is that whenever God, or life itself, issues the summons, it's normal to feel both unworthy and unprepared, but it doesn't matter. We are into the gap between our current capacity and what's needed anyway. When good things result, we know deep in our bones "that this extraordinary power belongs to God and does not come from us."[10]

Another compelling example is known as the miracle of the loaves and fish. One of the few stories that shows up in all four Gospel accounts, it tells of a time when Jesus and his disciples attempt to take some time away to rest, but thousands of people followed them to their place of seclusion. Jesus, in his compassion, set aside his fatigue and ministers to them and instructs his disciples to do the same. At the end of that long day, the disciples plead with Jesus to send the crowds home. "This is a deserted place and the hour is now very late," they say, "send them away so that they may go into the surrounding country and villages and buy something for themselves to eat."[11]

There are two versions of what happens next. In one, Jesus instructs the disciples to provide food for the people to eat. But they have only five loaves of bread and two fish. In the second version, a young boy offers his dinner—again, a few loaves and some fish. In both stories, Jesus takes what is offered, asks God's blessing, and gives the food back to the disciples to distribute to the crowds. There is enough for thousands to eat their fill, with twelve baskets filled with leftovers. "Gather up the fragments left over," Jesus instructs the disciples, "so that nothing may be lost."[12]

I live my entire life inside the miracle of the loaves and fish. Nearly every sermon I preach feels incomplete and inadequate, but I preach it anyway, praying that Jesus will fill in the gaps. My leadership is often imperfect and insufficient, but I lead to the best of my ability anyway and wait for Jesus to step in. The money I give away, particularly in response to acute human suffering, is never enough to meet the need, but I give anyway, hoping that, along with others, I might ease another's pain. The image of a few loaves and some fish feeding a multitude is meant to encourage us all to give what we have when we know it is not enough. For reasons beyond our understanding, God consistently chooses to work through our imperfect, inadequate offerings.

One summer when our boys were in elementary school, we came home from an extended vacation just in time for me to preside at worship on a Sunday morning. My sermon consisted of a few thoughts strung together at the last minute and a story about an orphaned girl from Russia whom we had recently met while staying with my grandparents in Sweden. This was the first summer after the collapse of the Soviet Union, and she was spending the summer with my grandparents' neighbors. I couldn't get her out of my mind, because while we were there, she clung to me as if I were her lost mother. I hated to say goodbye. It wasn't a particularly inspiring sermon, but it was all that I had.

A married couple who had joined the church a few months before was sitting in the back row. After church, they told me that my words inspired them to continue working through a challenging international adoption process. "We were at the point of giving up on our attempt to adopt two sisters from the former Soviet Union. When you spoke about the girl you met, it was as if God was telling us to persevere," they told me.

What's true in preaching is equally true in other contexts, for what we say even in seemingly casual conversation can have far greater impact than we realize. We may never know when our words, even those we thought were bumbling or inconsequential, were exactly what another person needed to hear and would have missed had we not spoken to them.

There is another side to the experience of inadequacy, however, one far more painful and humbling. When we step up and make our insufficient offering, typically there is no miracle, and the adverse consequences of our ill-preparedness and incompetence are there for all the world to see. How we respond in the face of failure is one of the most determinative decisions we make. If we can learn to accept failure as a part of growth, trusting that such experiences are part of a larger narrative of courage and purpose, we can glean the lessons we need to learn from the pain and move on. The next time it's our turn to step up, we are better prepared, and in retrospect, we see how essential failure is in learning to be brave.

A few years ago, I came across a short essay addressed to young artists written by Ira Glass, the host and executive producer of the popular radio show and podcast *This American Life*. He begins by acknowledging the initial distance between artistic aspiration and our first stuttering attempts to express it. "For the first couple years that you're making stuff, what you're making isn't so good," he writes. "What you're making is kind of a disappointment to you."[13] But what the artist does *next* determines everything:

> *If you are just starting out or if you are still in this phase, you gotta know it's normal and the most important thing you can do is do a lot of work.... It is only by going through a volume of work that you're going to catch up and close that gap. And the work you're making will be as good as your ambitions.*[14]

Stepping up to the plate when you aren't ready is the price of beginning. It's what you must do, time and again, when moving toward something important and becoming the person who is able to do or accomplish what is currently beyond your ability. You show up, take your place, step up to the plate, and swing and miss, and miss, and miss—until one day you make contact.

My public missteps have been among the most instructive, albeit painful, lessons in leadership. They have taught me humility. I've learned that facing my critics, taking in what they have to say and owning my mistakes, is not only the best way to ride out the storm but also to grow in maturity.

Three years into my role as bishop, I preached a Christmas Eve sermon at Washington National Cathedral that, to put it mildly, did not go well. Given the emotional intensity of the season and the fact that more people tend to show up in church, Christmas is a high-stress experience for most preachers. I feel that pressure every year, and even more acutely at the Cathedral because its service attracts large crowds, with many who haven't entered a church in years, if at all. Christmas Eve is my annual opportunity to share with a wide audience the most life-affirming message of the Christian faith: that God is love, and for love of humankind, God comes to us where we are, as we are. Given the Cathedral's location and audience, there is also an expectation to address the wider issues of the day. The stakes feel high every year.

I had done my best to prepare that year, but my offering, as Ira Glass would say, wasn't very good. I had no choice but to preach what I had and pray that it would be one of those times when the Spirit would make up for my lack of inspiration. It wasn't. Worse still, I managed to offend several Jewish attendees and their Christian friends with an example I used. Without intending to, I struck a nerve that shot pain through a large section of the Jewish community affiliated with the Cathedral. Some were perplexed and hurt. Others were furious.

Word spread, and by Christmas morning, my email inbox was filled with expressions of disappointment and outrage. One person went so far as to contact the religion editor of *The Washington Post* to complain about what I had said. I was mortified.

Several friends tried to make me feel better, going so far as to praise the sermon and dismiss as inconsequential the negative reactions it had evoked. A few took aim at my critics and encouraged me to ignore them. It was tempting to put the blame on those who came at me with such intensity. Part of a preacher's task, after all, is to risk making people uncomfortable when speaking painful but necessary truths. But that wasn't my intention. Instead, an illustration that, frankly, I hadn't given that much thought to was a source of offense and hurt for some who had come that night for inspiration and beauty. I felt terrible.

In the scheme of things, this was a relatively minor public misstep, and I have made far more spectacular ones since then. But at the time, I was completely undone. Preaching well matters to me, and not only had I disappointed those who were kind enough not to say anything, I had caused others genuine distress. The barrage of critique was overwhelming, and I was unprepared for the emotional spiral I went down during the next few days.

In a gift of providence, Dr. Brené Brown's book *Rising Strong: How the Ability to Reset Transforms the Way We Live, Love, Parent, and Lead* fell into my hands in those tumultuous days. It was a lifeline— eleven chapters on the pain and humiliation of failing in any realm of life, large or small, and how to recover from it. Brown refers to an image that defined her earlier work, that of an arena in which someone is willing to fail while daring greatly to achieve something. In *Rising Strong*, however, she lingers on the moment when that brave person has collapsed facedown. "Our 'facedown' moments can be big like getting fired or finding out about an affair," she writes, "or they can be small ones like learning a child has lied about her report card or experiencing disappointment at work."[15] I couldn't put the book down.

As she has done for so many, Brown gave me permission to face the pain of public criticism and personal disappointment and to learn its lessons well. In those pages, she challenged me to do the work: "To pretend that we can get to *helping, generous,* and *brave* without navigating through tough emotions like *desperation, shame,* and *panic* is a profoundly dangerous and misguided assumption."[16]

Reading her words felt like a crucible moment: what kind of public leader would I be?

Brown outlines a simple, yet challenging process for rising when we fall, or as I've come to experience it, stepping up *again*, this time into the moment presented by having previously stepped up and failed. First there is "reckoning," when we take stock of where we find ourselves, acknowledging the hurt and disorientation of falling, and moving from judgment to curiosity."[17] Next there is the "rumble," where we truly own what has happened and ask the questions that broaden our understanding. Finally, there is the "revolution"— a term Brown uses to convey the kind of bold transformation that can occur in individuals and society when we become the kind of people who are willing to fail for the things that matter, precisely because we know we can rise again.[18]

I decided to send a personal apology to all who had written to me of their hurt and anger and offer to meet. Nearly everyone wrote back, surprised and appreciative that I had contacted them. Four accepted my invitation, and in the new year, I welcomed each one into my office. I listened to their stories, which helped me better understand why my words had been so offensive. I didn't agree with every point they made, but I was reminded of the power of language to trigger pain. Our differences mattered less than the fact that we were talking about tender issues of faith and identity.

I also discovered that I could step up to the plate of turmoil that I had created, and in doing so, diffuse a volatile situation. In *Love Is the Way*, Bishop Curry writes about "learning how to stand and kneel at the same time," that is, holding true to his convictions while receiving anger from another person with compassion and respect.[19] It was critical for me to allow those I had hurt to express their anger, take it in, and remain standing. It is a lesson I must relearn with every failure, both public and private.

I wish I could say that failing gets easier, but it hurts just as much each time. Still, there is no other way I would rather live or lead. That's the revolutionary part, Brown argues: "When the process becomes *a practice* [italics mine]—a way of engaging the world— there's no doubt that it ignites revolutionary change. It changes us and it changes the people around us."[20]

A third and perhaps the most faith-affirming way we experience the call to step up is when we are feeling mired in the complexity and contradictions of our lives. To be summoned out of the quagmire of self-absorption to do something brave and good in a completely different sphere is sheer grace. It's a relief to think about something else and reconnect with all that gives life meaning precisely when we feel least worthy of it.

The classic example comes from the patriarch Jacob, whose story is told in the Book of Genesis. A word of warning for those who haven't read the early biblical texts: much of what we find there is offensive to modern sensibilities. In the ancient world, slavery, polygamy, patriarchy, and violence were normative, and like some in our time, many people, including those writing these texts, believed that such atrocities were God-sanctioned.

Fortunately, there is a corrective thread throughout Scripture and an admirable willingness to acknowledge the failures and sins of our spiritual ancestors. In other words, the Bible tells stories of imperfect human beings and their encounters with God through sweeps of history that are as messy as our own time. As each generation reads the ancient texts through a new lens, they reveal fresh insights that provide meaning, challenge, consolation, and guidance. I am among those who believe that through the texts, God speaks to those who choose to listen.

Back to Jacob, who, by all accounts, is a scoundrel and thief. As a young man, he steals his older brother Esau's birthright and then proceeds to cheat Esau out of their father's blessing—a particular ritual of the ancient world that could only be bestowed once. At his mother's urging, Jacob leaves home, ostensibly to find a wife among their kinsmen in another region, but equally important, to escape Esau's rage.

Jacob meets his match in his future father-in-law, Laban, himself an opportunist. After a love-at-first-sight encounter with Laban's youngest daughter, Rachel, Jacob asks for Laban's blessing to marry her. Laban agrees, provided that Jacob works for him for seven years. But after Jacob completes his side of the arrangement, Laban tricks him into marrying Rachel's older sister, Leah, assuring Joseph that after seven more years' labor, he can marry Rachel as well. Jacob agrees and eventually is married to both daughters. Jacob prospers in his father-in-law's household, so much so that Laban and his sons become suspicious of him and their relationship sours.

Amid this family drama, God speaks to Jacob: "Return to the land of your ancestors and to your kindred, and I will be with you."[21] It is as clear a call as Abraham had received before him, and he, too, answers without hesitation. He conspires with both his wives to plan their escape. They slip away early one morning, taking with them all that they can carry, including the sacred objects in Laban's household.

On his way back to his homeland, Jacob's past returns to haunt him, as he rightfully worries about how Esau will receive him. After sending a peace offering, Jacob hears word that his brother is coming to meet him, accompanied by four hundred men. Now Jacob is truly frightened.

After sending his family ahead for protection, Jacob waits alone for his brother to arrive. Here the story shifts into a mystical realm. Out of the darkness a stranger appears and attacks him, and they wrestle all night. Jacob seems resigned, but he keeps fighting. At one point, the man strikes Jacob's hip, seriously wounding him, but Jacob does not relent. At sunrise, the stranger pleads with Jacob to let him go. "I will not let you go," Jacob replies, "unless you bless me." "You shall no longer be called Jacob," the stranger says to him, "for you have striven with God and with humans and have prevailed."[22]

We come to realize alongside Jacob that he had been wrestling all night with God. "I have seen God face to face, and yet my life is preserved," he marvels afterward. The blessing he asked for and received was his alone, supplanting the blessing he had stolen from his brother. The next day Jacob and Esau meet and reconcile. As an acknowledgment of the blessing's cost, Jacob limps for the rest of his life.

What strikes me here isn't Jacob's deviousness, which remains a constant, but that time and again, God looks past his selfish, deceptive actions and calls him to take his place in the lineage of God's people. In a compelling sermon preached at Washington National Cathedral on September 27, 2020, Archbishop of Canterbury Justin

Welby dwells on the story of Jacob, describing him as "the lonely victim of self-imposed family trauma, the narcissistic con man."

> *He has cheated his father and his brother, yet God's grace and love are greater than his sins and failing. He is in great danger, hot pursuit, his coast behind him, wild animals all around him. Yet God, the God of his ancestors, is with him. In Jacob's ignorance and sin, God draws near. Rescues, blesses, sets him on a new course. His future is a blessing received and given. There is no simple solution. Virtue is not rewarded nor sin punished. There is no comfortable sense that because he is blessed, he was therefore right. God's grace is lavish, but it also demands that we give all that we are. Before Jacob, in his future, as well as a blessing of 14 years of growling and underpaid labor, he will live by his which he will cheat again. Yet God's grace remains lavish.*[23]

The archbishop encapsulates God's way of calling us out of ourselves: "Jacob's complexity of action and motivation is met in God, not by simplifying or condoning, but by calling."[24] God doesn't excuse, condone, or seem bothered by Jacob's past. God merely picks him up out of his morass and sets him on a different path, giving him something worthy to do.

I've lost count of the times I have been rescued from the downward spiral of my thoughts, anxieties, or foolish actions by the call to step up to something else. That pivot doesn't take away or solve my life's ambiguities and contradictions, but for a time, I'm lifted out of them, free to focus my attention on something worthwhile, to do something for someone else.

In early September of 2021, I felt sadness to the point of despair washing over me. The end of summer is often a time of melancholy for me and that year it was particularly intense. We had said good-bye to our adult children and sweet toddler grandchildren, not knowing, given pandemic precautions, when we would be able to see them again. I faced the prospect of returning to work after several weeks away where multiple tasks were waiting, none that I wanted to do. It was as pure a depressive state as I've experienced in some time, and I was perfectly content to sink further down.

Then I remembered that a neighbor was organizing what she called a "yard giveaway" (as opposed to a yard sale) that weekend to help immigrant families who had been particularly hard hit by the pandemic and subsequent economic shutdown. Feeling weary, I almost let the opportunity to help pass by, but late one night I packed up our car with dishes, pots and pans, blankets, clothes, and furniture. The next morning, I drove to the site of the giveaway, a basketball court near a large apartment complex in a part of the city I had never been to before.

On the basketball court, a dozen or so volunteers were organizing a mountain of donations into what looked like the first floor of a department store while a line formed outside. Children ran around the perimeter, pointing excitedly to the bicycles and toys. When the gate opened, it felt like Christmas morning.

My job was to escort elderly residents as they made their selections. One woman, whom I learned was suffering from cancer, asked me to hold her bag. As we walked through each station, I watched teenage girls try on jackets and pass pairs of jeans between them, seeking the right fit. Younger children held stuffed animals. Couples carried furniture back to their apartments. As the court emptied of goods and people, I spoke with the women who had organized the event. They were tired and gratified, and already making plans for their next effort.

What I gave away from our household and my presence at the gathering were of modest help that day, but what I received was a priceless gift. Simply being in a community that was practicing love raised me out of my crippling sadness to a space of gratitude. When the giveaway was over, I was still the same person with the same struggles. But joining in the act of neighborliness allowed me, for a time, to break free. It was a grace-filled reminder of God, who sees all my brokenness and responds not by simplifying or condoning, but by inviting me to step out of myself and into something worthwhile. Whenever it happens, I am, like Jacob, grateful for God's willingness to work through my imperfections. It's not a matter of being good enough for God or anyone else, but of answering the summons that beckons us on.

───────

Those whose stories I've been privileged to share in this book all had their "step up to the plate" moments, some of personal significance, and others with a societal impact reverberating across time. One reason I am captivated by the struggle for racial justice and civil rights in this country is because the historical narrative ties together so many of those courageous moments, as individuals make possible what has long seemed beyond reach and inspire future generations to carry forward the dream. My focus has been primarily on personal stories, but the collective account is equally powerful. For when brave souls come together in common purpose, led by those who helped them believe that their contribution matters, the world changes for the better.

Let's return to the triumphant moment in 1965 when Martin Luther King Jr. spoke from the steps of the state capitol building in Montgomery, Alabama, for it was the hard-won fruit of countless acts of courage. The resistance to voting rights for Black persons in Alabama (indeed, for civil rights of any kind) had been fierce and ugly. The journey to Montgomery began in bloodshed, when, on March 7, marchers had been violently turned back on the Edmund Pettus Bridge. Thanks to the presence of television cameras, the nation witnessed the carnage, and King seized the moment. He wasn't in Montgomery on what is now known as "Bloody Sunday," but he led a second attempt to cross the bridge two days later, defying local edicts outlawing the march. Moreover, he called upon white clergy and people of goodwill from around the country to join him in peaceful protest. Hundreds immediately made their way south, including Washington National Cathedral Dean Francis B. Sayre Jr.

After days of negotiation and local demonstrations, a federal judge granted protection for a limited number of people to make the journey, and the fifty-four-mile walk to Montgomery began in earnest. At every turn, local authorities and white vigilante groups threatened the marchers with violence. Television cameras and journalists joined the five-day pilgrimage, as did National Guard troops, there to protect the marchers. Thousands of Black men and women from across Alabama risked their lives and their livelihoods to meet King on the road. The power of the march lay in the number of people willing to put their bodies on the line.

One such man was a Black railroad worker named Henry Caffey, who lived in the small town of Trickem, Alabama. Caffey had worked for the railroad all his life as a "gandy dancer," laying, straightening, and repairing sections of track by hand. By 1965, Henry had risen to the rank of section master, the highest position to which a Black man could aspire in his field. He was a respected employee and on good terms with most of the white men for whom he worked. Henry's teenage daughter wanted to join the march as it passed near Trickem.

I learned the story of Henry Caffey and his daughter from my colleague Andrew Waldo, who grew up in Montgomery in the 1960s, the son of an Episcopal priest. As a boy, Andrew had played with the children of civil rights leaders, both Black and white, and he's always been passionately interested in trains and how the railroads shaped our nation's history. One year on sabbatical, Andrew returned to Montgomery to interview as many of the retired workers of the Western Railway of Alabama whom he could find. One afternoon, he sat on Caffey's front porch, listening to the old man reminisce about those turbulent years.

The Selma to Montgomery march was a stepping-up moment of enormous consequence, certainly for the young girl, but also for her father. As Andrew put it, "In a small Alabama town, everybody knows everybody. If she took part in the march, everybody would know, and somebody would pay." I imagine quite a father-daughter conversation, but like many whose courageous acts we witness, all I know is that in the end, Caffey agreed to drive her to join the march. As they made their way on the three-mile road between their home and the highway, a state trooper recognized Caffey's car and pulled him over. The officer wrote a ticket and said, "Henry, take your daughter back home, and I'll tear up this ticket." Caffey replied, "You can write up as many tickets as you want. My daughter's going to march in that march."[25]

Among the white clergy traveling south was an Episcopal seminary student from Cambridge, Massachusetts, named Jonathan Daniels. Daniels shared the idealistic aspirations of many young Northerners, and he had become awakened to America's harsh racial disparities through an urban ministry internship in Providence, Rhode Island. His decision to go to Selma nonetheless came as a surprise to him because, earlier that same year, he had publicly defended the Episcopal bishop of Alabama, who had explicitly told Northern Episcopalians to stay out of his jurisdiction.[26]

Daniels was among a group of seminarians who, on March 7, watched the carnage on the Edmund Pettus Bridge on live television. When he heard King's plea for religious leaders to come South, Daniels decided to raise money to help other students make the journey rather than go himself. At that evening's chapel service, however, as Daniels joined in singing what's known as the *Magnificat*, or Mary's Song, he had what can only be described as a conversion experience, as the mother of Jesus urged him to go to Selma.[27]

Daniels and his companions were among the two thousand peaceful protestors who marched with Dr. King through downtown Selma, but after they crossed the Edmund Pettus Bridge, they were abruptly stopped by a federal court order. At this stage in the Civil Rights Movement, King would not defy the federal government, their only real protection against southern extremism. Many who came to march returned home in disappointment.

Feeling uneasy with such a short and fruitless witness, Daniels and his seminary classmate Judy Upham chose to stay in Selma. Alongside them was the Reverend James Reeb, a Unitarian minister from Boston, who had been on the same flight as Daniels. That evening, Reeb was attacked and killed by white vigilantes as he was leaving a Black restaurant, his death sending a chilling message to everyone who remained: they, too, were risking their lives.

After President Johnson delivered a speech to a joint session of Congress in support of the Voting Rights Bill, King finally secured federal permission and promises of protection. Daniels and Upham were then among the more than three thousand people who walked out of Selma on the first day. From there, only three hundred people were authorized to continue on the narrow highway that led to Montgomery. Daniels helped shuttle people back to Selma, and he returned each night to set up campsites and keep guard. The crowds returned for the final stretch five days later. Daniels and Upham were there on March 25 to hear King's jubilant speech as twenty thousand people stood with him before the state capitol.

As the marchers hurried to leave Montgomery before nightfall, Viola Liuzzo, a thirty-nine-year-old white woman who had driven down from Detroit to participate, was bringing a group of students back to Selma on a desolate stretch of Highway 80 when a car filled with Klansmen sped past her car. One man rolled down his window, aimed a gun, and shot her dead.[28] Sobered by Liuzzo's death, inspired by the courageous witness of so many, and having fallen in love with the Black family who took them into their home, Daniels and Upham stayed in Selma all spring, registering voters, and tutoring elementary school students. Daniels also served on a dialogue committee with prominent white leaders in Selma, including members of the local Episcopal Church, many of whom were resistant to integration of their congregation.

By then, the national spotlight had left Selma, as King focused his energies elsewhere and racial tensions flared in northern cities. But Daniels's sense of vocation had been fixed ever since the night he sang *Magnificat* in the chapel. As Stephanie Spellers writes in her book *The Church Cracked Open: Disruption, Decline, and New Hope for Beloved Community*, "Mary's revolutionary cry helped turn Daniels's face toward Selma."[29] And there he stayed.

Daniels and Upham returned to seminary for final exams, and by July, Daniels was back in Alabama to devote the entire summer to activism and voter registration, one of only a handful of white civil rights workers in the state. Camera and notebook in hand, he was determined to document the abject poverty and abusive treatment Black residents endured and, in whatever ways he could, improve them. If conditions were poor in Selma, they were even worse in the neighboring Lowndes County, the poorest in the state. There, Black people outnumbered white people four to one, and most worked as sharecroppers on former plantations under conditions not much better than in the days of slavery. Segregation was uncompromisingly cruel. Black residents who tried to vote were refused, or subjected to literacy tests, and often fired from their jobs afterward.

Far from the national spotlight, Stokely Carmichael and the Student Nonviolent Coordinating Committee (SNCC) were making slow inroads through painstaking organizing efforts in Lowndes County, and Daniels wanted to be among them. John Lewis, at the time the national chairman of SNCC, would later say of Daniels that he had become like kin to the county's Black farmers and a leader in his own right.[30]

History was made on August 6, when President Johnson signed into law the Voting Rights Act of 1965. Federal voting registrars soon began arriving in Lowndes County. Meanwhile, national attention was fixed on California, where the largest Black rebellion since World War II broke out in the Watts neighborhood of Los Angeles. The mood among white residents in Lowndes County grew more ominous as they feared a similar uprising. "Whites who for generations had with impunity used violence against Blacks would only expect that Blacks would return the violence," writes Charles Eagles in his biography of Jonathan Daniels. "At the same time, the nation's response to the Watts riots convinced Lowndes white supremacists that they had widespread public support in combating Black insurrection."[31] In such a charged, paranoid environment, the simple act of registering to vote was considered a threat to white social control.

Many Black students, too young to vote yet determined to be heard, stepped up to the plate. Working with SNCC organizers in early August, a group of students planned a protest in the predominantly white town of Fort Deposit, Alabama, where Black customers were often denied service in the local stores or charged significantly higher prices. Local SNCC leaders communicated their fears of Klansmen retaliation to their headquarters in Atlanta and asked for police protection and press coverage. John Lewis sent a telegram to Governor George Wallace demanding protection for the demonstrators, to no avail.[32]

When the white community heard of the planned protest, they armed themselves as if preparing for war. "Rumors circulated among bewildered, fearful white residents that freedom riders had come to Fort Deposit," Eagles writes. "Armed whites patrolled the town in angry anticipation. Guns and clubs were evident everywhere."[33] Around 10 a.m., a few Black adults made their way into town and stood in front of the post office, waiting to register to vote. Meanwhile, the young people planned to begin their demonstration from the Methodist church north of town.

Daniels, along with a Catholic priest named Richard Morrisroe, decided to support the teenagers in their first protest. By now, such stepping up was second nature for Daniels. Those present in Fort Deposit that day remember him as relaxed, seeming to enjoy himself as he marched through town. In groups of eight to ten, Black youth and young adults walked up to three offending stores carrying signs of protest. They were peaceful and orderly, yet as an armed group of white men approached, the Fort Deposit police arrested all the demonstrators, including Daniels and Morrisroe.

Everyone over the age of eighteen spent six miserable days in jail in the nearby town of Hayneville, as lawyers and activists from across Alabama tried to secure their release. Then, on August 20, without explanation, they were told to leave town immediately. Daniels, Morrisroe, and two other protestors, Ruby Sales and Joyce Bailey, decided to stop and buy soft drinks in the one store in Hayneville where Black people could shop freely. Unbeknownst to them, a white man named Tom Coleman had received word from the sheriff's office about the released civil rights workers and had driven ahead to the store. As Daniels opened the screen door for Sales to enter, Coleman appeared with his shotgun and yelled for them to leave. In the final stepping up of his life, Daniels pushed Sales out of the way. Coleman shot him point blank in the chest.

On the mantel in my office, I have a replica of the stone carving of Jonathan Daniels that can be found in the Human Rights Porch of Washington National Cathedral. People often ask me who he is, and I gladly tell the story of a young man who learned how to be brave. Courage cost him his life, yet it also taught him how to live.

Although our stepping-up moments may seem small by comparison, they have a cumulative effect, and there may be far more at stake every time we choose to step up than we realize. We're never more alive than when we take our turn at the most necessary things, fulfill the deeper purposes of our lives, and know ourselves to be accepted despite our failings and called to do something brave.

CHAPTER SIX

The Inevitable Letdown

No good deed goes unpunished.

—Oscar Wilde[1]

The Christian season of Lent, which calls us into self-reflection and amendment of life, is patterned on an intense time of trial and temptation that Jesus experienced immediately after his baptism by John in the Jordan River. The juxtaposition is striking. No sooner does the Spirit of God speak to Jesus as he rises from the waters of baptism, saying, "You are my Son, the Beloved; with you I am well pleased," than that same Spirit *drives* him into the wilderness to be tempted by Satan.[2] In one moment, Jesus is basking in the affirmation of God; in the next, he is contending with his human frailties in a mighty struggle against the force of evil. If Jesus had any delusions of grandeur, they were dashed in the wilderness.

Such is the emotional whiplash that follows many a decisive moment. I've counseled more than one couple preparing for marriage through an intense, though typically short-lived, crisis when one or both of the outwardly happy pair were having second thoughts. After the euphoria of becoming engaged, doubts plagued them as the reality of what they were about to commit to sank in. Similarly, during the experience of childbirth, which many people describe as the most powerful spiritual moment of their lives, there is a predictable swing of intense emotion from euphoria to exhaustion-induced depression, an overwhelming and guilt-inducing experience for new parents who haven't yet learned that such feelings are normal. Although circumstances vary, the inevitable emotional letdown that follows a decisive moment can throw us off course and cause us to question the validity or lasting power of what we had thought to be a transformative experience.

One minor example from my life often comes to mind when I need reminding of what it feels like to hold steady in the often-fragile emotional state that awaits on the other side of courage. During my last year of seminary, I was struggling with indecision about the trajectory of my coursework. The choice before me was between a more traditional track of study and one with a much greater sense of adventure. The traditional classes would be more demanding academically and serve to keep me on campus. The more adventuresome option would involve commuting into Washington, D.C., each week and taking my place among others who felt called to the gritty world of urban ministry. I had enough perspective to realize that this wasn't a life-or-death decision. Nonetheless, I was truly stuck.

I went for a swim at the local recreation center with this quandary on my mind. As I was doing laps, clarity finally came, like the proverbial lightbulb I had been praying for. I knew without a doubt that the best decision was to stay on campus, focus on essentials, and enjoy the last weeks at seminary. Relief energized me, and I finished my workout strong and confident. But no sooner had I stepped out of the pool and begun to dry off than all the uncertainty returned, overtaking the confidence I had felt just moments before. The letdown came so quickly that I burst out laughing. Then it dawned on me that I could either trust what had happened in the pool or heed the rush of doubt that followed. In what felt like an act of faith, I chose to go with my experience in the water. The decision itself has long since faded in significance, yet the memory of receiving the gift of clarity followed by an immediate sense that it was an illusion has helped me navigate the same swing of emotion when the stakes have been much higher.

Letdown comes in many forms. After the rush of energy dissipates, the most predictable feeling is *emptiness*, as life, in all its ambiguity, snaps back into place. Old routines and unresolved issues reassert themselves. Doubt rushes in. For a time, we lose our bearings and are tempted to retreat from the path of courage, or, equally dangerous, veer into overconfidence, with a temporary sense of invincibility blinding us to what's up ahead.

The Gospels share a pointed example of that latter dynamic in an exchange between Jesus and his disciple Simon Peter. As Jesus' ministry is gathering momentum and his celebrity status rising, he takes those closest to him aside to ponder what it all means. "Who do the people say that the Son of Man is?" he asks them. "Some say John the Baptist," they reply, a remarkable statement given that John, the leader of the spiritual movement from which Jesus emerged, had recently been executed by King Herod. "But others Elijah," they continue, referring to an ancient prophet who, in Jewish lore, was thought to return as a forerunner to the Messiah. "Still others Jeremiah or one of the prophets."[3] Jesus is obviously stirring hope among the populace and igniting dreams of liberation from the Roman occupation.

Jesus then asks, "But who do *you* say that I am?" With immediate and astonishing clarity, Simon Peter declares, "You are the Messiah, the Son of the living God." Deeply moved, Jesus exclaims, "Blessed are you, Simon son of Jonah! For flesh and blood has not revealed this to you, but my Father in heaven. . . . You are Peter [a name derived from the Greek *petra*, meaning 'stone'], and on this rock I will build my church."[4] To Simon Peter's astonishment, and surely all the others, Jesus elevated him to a position of leadership.

If only the conversation had ended there. But Jesus continues, swearing the disciples to silence, telling them that he is destined to suffer and die when they enter Jerusalem. Simon Peter protests, "God forbid it, Lord! This must never happen to you." Jesus' rebuke is immediate: "Get behind me, Satan! You are a stumbling block to me, for you are setting your mind not on divine things but on human things." Seconds after hearing Jesus' highest praise, Simon Peter is humiliated in front of his peers.[5]

Like Simon Peter, I have sometimes mistakenly assumed, in the afterglow of public praise, that an accomplishment or insight in one realm of my life would carry into others. Once, for example, when I was parish priest in Minneapolis, I became involved in a faith-based community organization known as ISAIAH, a multiracial, nonpartisan coalition dedicated to racial and economic justice in Minnesota.[6] Periodically, the leaders of ISAIAH would invite me to be one of the speakers at a community gathering or the lead organizer of a meeting with elected officials. These efforts required significant preparation and practice, and the events themselves were often thrilling. I loved speaking before a crowd or firmly advocating a position within the halls of political power. On occasion, I was effective enough to garner attention and public acclaim.

Invariably, after a meeting or event in which I played a leading role, another group or community organizer would invite me to speak out on a different issue or take part in another action for which I was not prepared. Basking in my earlier success, I would say yes. Suffice to say, the results were always embarrassing. I would feel chastened and exposed as the political novice that I was. "Never let mistakes stop you," a community organizer once counseled after he watched me retreat after a disastrous meeting with an elected official. "Learn everything you can from this and carry on."

Back to the exchange between Jesus and Simon Peter: it's noteworthy that Jesus' rebuke doesn't cause him to change his mind about Simon Peter's future leadership. And although Jesus' words must have stung, Simon Peter remains at his side. Nor would this be the last time he would fail Jesus. The most excruciating incident was yet to come, after Jesus was arrested, when Simon Peter publicly denies knowing him three times. When Jesus is crucified, Simon Peter and the other male disciples flee in fear, while the women of their group remain at the cross.

In one Gospel account, the men return to their home villages and their old jobs as fishermen, paralyzed with grief. Then one day the resurrected Jesus appears, waiting on the shore for them as they bring in their night catch. Overtaken with emotion, Simon Peter jumps into the water and swims ashore. "Come and have breakfast,"

Jesus says to them. He then assures Simon Peter that he not only is forgiven, but also still called to lead. Simon Peter picks himself up and keeps going.[7]

I suppose that it shouldn't have come as a surprise that I'd experience a public fall from grace while still on the receiving end of effusive public admiration for my stance against former President Trump. The esteem certainly wasn't universal, but among the people whose opinion of my work matters to me, my public stature had risen considerably. The praise was both affirming and seductive. I was invited to speak on podcasts and write op-eds for national newspapers. The organizers of the 2020 Democratic National Convention asked me to offer a benediction. Organizations around the country invited me to preach or lead seminars. In late January 2021, I was featured in a church publication extolling my leadership.[8]

Then in February 2021, a decision that I made with my colleague, the Very Reverend Randolph Marshall Hollerith, dean of Washington National Cathedral, prompted such harsh and sustained public critique that for several weeks I wasn't sure if my episcopate would survive. We were still in the early period of pandemic lockdown, months before vaccinations were available. Washington National Cathedral was enjoying a national wave of public gratitude for its high-quality online worship that provided a spiritual lifeline for thousands of homebound people across the country. The Dean had begun inviting prominent clergy from a variety of traditions and theological perspectives to record sermons later aired as part of the Cathedral's virtual Sunday worship. Most of the guest speakers were well received. But on the Friday morning before a prominent evangelical Christian preacher and author, Max Lucado, was scheduled to preach, Randy called me, and I knew why.

By then I had noticed word that Lucado would be speaking from the Cathedral's pulpit had prompted alarm on social media platforms because of statements he had made in the past against LGBTQ+ persons. Soon there was an organized effort to convince Randy and me to rescind the invitation. We both considered ourselves strong allies of LGBTQ+ members of the church and assumed that our solidarity was not in question. In a phrase I have often used in attempting to lead across differences, I thought that "we could afford to be generous" with those who held other views, to create civil discourse on contentious topics. "Who are you asking to be generous?" one person shot back. "Would you ask Black Christians to be generous in listening to a white supremacist?"

The Dean and I watched Lucado's prerecorded sermon. His topic was on the power of the Holy Spirit in our lives with no mention of his views on human sexuality, and we didn't think it would cause offense. Moreover, Lucado had privately expressed to Dean Hollerith his regret for the insensitivity of the remarks he had made years before, likening gay sex to bestiality. We decided to air his sermon.

The public outcry was overwhelming. For days, my inbox was flooded with hundreds of emails expressing hurt, anger, and confusion. In anguish, people asked why we had ceded the Cathedral pulpit, our most esteemed public platform, to someone who refused to renounce the cruel statements that he had made and whose church was not a welcoming place for LGBTQ+ persons. Some wrote long paragraphs, recounting childhood memories of having

Max Lucado's words read to them by their parents and pastors; of being rejected by their congregations when they came out as gay or lesbian; of living in fear for their transgender children and grandchildren. The letters were heartbreaking. When I tried to express my rationale in a social media post, it only made things worse.

The intensity of the emotions coming toward us—confusion, disappointment, grief, and rage—stopped me cold. LGBTQ+ members of the Cathedral congregation asked in disbelief why we hadn't consulted them. The leadership bodies of the diocese wondered the same thing, and many clergy felt personally betrayed. I also caused a pastoral crisis for many in their congregations, they told me, as yet again I had asked those most harmed by the church's bigotry to pay the larger price in the interest of building relationships with evangelical Christians. People across the country demanded to know how we decided, and when, and what the process was for vetting cathedral preachers. Our most vocal critics called into question our commitment to justice, interpreting past decisions in light of this one.

Not all the feedback was critical. Some people wrote to say that we had done the right thing by not bowing to public pressure and that the whole affair was an example of our society's toxic polarity, intolerance, and cancel culture. Their words were intended to reassure us, but they didn't. They may even be true, but the fact remained that I had hurt people I loved and caused many to question whether the Episcopal Church was a safe spiritual home for them.

There was nothing I could do except the painstaking work of apology and restitution. Past mistakes had taught me the steps, but knowledge didn't make it easier. For a solid week while I was in quarantine at an Airbnb in Minneapolis (waiting for a clear COVID-19 test so that I might hold our newborn granddaughter), I rose each day alone and responded to every angry and hurt email.

Thus began tentative dialogues with those among my critics willing to engage. Many were not, but some did graciously, including the mother of a transgender child who told me that she worried for their life every day and LGBTQ+ colleagues who asked if I thought they would ever be welcome to speak in Max Lucado's church. I had humbling conversations with friends who assured me of their love, but that they needed me to know how much I had hurt them. The presiding bishop was pastorally supportive, but also clear that Randy and I needed to make a public apology, which we did several times. Max Lucado also apologized in writing to us for past statements he had made that had caused so much pain. He did not, however, move away from his church's position against the full acceptance and inclusion of LGBTQ+ persons.

But apology wasn't enough, which was evident the evening we convened an online dialogue in which several hundred Episcopalians from across the country expressed their views on the incident. Dr. Kelly Brown Douglas, the Cathedral's canon theologian, acted as facilitator, a generous gesture given how disappointed she was in our actions. Others helped us strategize how to balance the need to listen with the need to answer questions. What we heard underscored how little I understood about the lived experience of LGBTQ+ persons and their families, and how sometimes the worst pain is inflicted upon them by those who imagine, as I did, that we were incapable of such harm. After ninety minutes on Zoom, the event ended without a sense of resolution. The social media conversation continued for days, and as hard as it was being the subject of criticism and speculation, I stayed in it as best I could.

The ordeal was a sober lesson in how quickly I could lose the trust that had taken years to establish and how much work would be required to build it back again. It also was painfully obvious that past actions of courageous leadership granted no immunity from the consequences of a public mistake. But I also needed to move on. A colleague whose public persona is stronger than mine texted me: "Chin up!" I wrote back words that I hoped were true: "While I'm not made of stone, I'm not made of glass either." Another colleague advised Randy and me when we were both feeling bruised and weary, "It's always harder being criticized by your allies. Don't let this stop you. Take the hit and get back up."

Eventually the storm blew over, and I settled back into the more natural state of doing my work without public notice. But for months I had the same feeling that I have after a near accident (or an actual one) when riding my bicycle. Our blind spots are dangerous precisely because we can't see them. On my bike, and in life, I'm particularly vulnerable to a fall when I feel on top of the world.

Letdowns are inevitable, but they do not have the final word unless we let them. Nor do they cancel out the initial gift of motivating insight that seems so far away when, in Brené Brown's words, "We're face down in the arena."[9] Still, it does take time to recover from the disorientation. We need to be honest with ourselves and others when we make a mistake or are brought to our knees. It's a way of living and leading with an undefended heart, truly open to others, and with a spine strong enough to withstand the experience, learn from it, and carry on.

There are relational and societal dimensions that contribute to letdown after an experience of courage or clarity that have more to do with the people around us than with ourselves. My teachers in family emotional process jokingly called this *payback*, and much of it is simply the price of being in a relationship with others. When our sons were young, for example, I came to expect payback from being away for any length of time; the house would be a disaster, the boys cranky, and Paul not particularly interested in hearing what had happened to me while he was tending to things at home. I felt hurt, but they were the ones who bore the brunt of my going, and I needed to allow them their emotions. I recognized the same behavior in myself whenever Paul went away for an extended bird-watching expedition or was given greater responsibilities in his work that took him away from us.

Payback is not an easy dynamic to navigate, and it varies in intensity depending on the emotional maturity of those involved and the level of change required by one person's decisive experience. Sensitivity to one another goes a long way in easing the tension of reentry, as do expressions of gratitude for the sacrifices others have made. It helps to listen to their time in the valley before describing ours on the mountain.

There are more damaging expressions of payback, however, which cross over into emotional abuse when unequal power dynamics are in play: a parent preventing a child from pursuing her dream that would take her away from the family, a coach holding back a gifted athlete because of his race, partners preventing or sabotaging one another's progress for fear of being left behind, a teacher inexplicably humiliating a promising student in front of their peers.

In my first job out of seminary, I worked as an assistant priest at Trinity Episcopal Church in Toledo, Ohio, alongside a priest named Walter Sobol, who had a reputation, as my bishop had warned me, "for having trouble working with women." I wasn't sure what that meant, but I was determined to be the exception to that rule. To his credit, Walter hired me when I was nine months' pregnant and gave me a position with considerable responsibility and freedom. But he never was comfortable with my success and with the congregation's growing affection for me. I came to expect humiliation whenever I accomplished something of significance or was publicly praised. Payback would come in the form of an insult to my appearance (or overly sexualized praise); a harsh critique of a sermon or something else I had done; or, after he knew my vulnerabilities, a carefully placed comment intended to unnerve me.

Because Walter could also be encouraging and overtly supportive of my ministry, these experiences of payback were doubly unnerving. After some time had passed, he would revert to his public stance of affection and praise. Whenever I mustered my courage to speak to him about something hurtful that he had said or done, he feigned ignorance or suggested that I was overreacting. It was crazy-making. I spent three years doubting my perceptions of what was happening and trying to be good enough to please him, without being so good as to overshadow his oversized ego.

My point here is that what we can experience as a letdown or payback—in my case, the push and pull I experienced each time I inadvertently ran afoul of my boss in my achievements—is as much relational as it is personal. Stepping out in courage affects the homeostasis of relationships and the communal structures upon which they depend. Even in our most loving relationships, we bear the cost of disruption in the patterns we've come to expect from one another. Decisive moments also can trigger the worst in human behavior, when one person, or group, or indeed the entire society, seeks to undermine or prevent the life-affirming progress of others.

Backlash is the sociological term to describe the harsh, often violent reaction against real or perceived advances for more expansive political and civil rights and other measures of social equality. The word came into popular usage in the early 1960s to describe the fierce white opposition to gains made by Black Americans during the Civil Rights Movement. But as historian Lawrence Glickman observes, backlash describes "one of the oldest and deepest patterns in American politics, signifying a virulent counter reaction to all manner of social movements and cultural transformations."[10]

Journalist and author Ta-Nehisi Coates's essay compilation *We Were Eight Years in Power: An American Tragedy* is a particularly compelling study of white backlash in which he draws haunting parallels between Barack Obama's two-term presidency and the post–Civil War Reconstruction Era—both historical moments of exemplary Black leadership that prompted ferocious opposition among the white populace. The title refers to a speech that South Carolina

Congressman Thomas Miller gave in 1885 in which he described all the good that had been done during the eight years that Black politicians controlled the legislature during Reconstruction. He pleaded with his white colleagues not to disenfranchise Black citizens, to no avail. Racial discrimination was codified in the new state constitution, as it was throughout the South. Where legal measures failed, they gave way to more violent means to maintain white rule.[11] Beyond making the obvious case for interpreting the election of Donald Trump through the lens of backlash to the Obama years, Coates traces the legacy of white supremacy from the Civil War forward and our proclivity as a nation to, at shining moments, "reach for the best part of itself, only to quickly retrench to the worst part of itself."[12]

Coates describes himself as one who would like to believe in God but can't, having learned at a young age that no god would save him from the brutality of this world.[13] Instead, he has found spiritual meaning in his family, work, and ancestry, and in telling Black history that "does not flatter American democracy, but chastens it."[14] I am drawn to Coates's writing for its poetic brilliance and historical narrative, but also because he finds the same call in atheism that I hear as a Christian to pursue the truth no matter where it leads and to live with hope grounded in things as they are. "I don't ever want to lose sight of how short my time is here," he writes. "I don't ever want to forget that resistance must be its own reward, since resistance, at least within the lifespan of the resistors, almost always fails . . . And if tragedy is to be proven wrong, if there really is hope out there, I think it can only be made manifest by remembering the cost of it being proven right."[15]

We live with the reverberations of societal backlash on so many fronts, yet we simply cannot afford to collapse in despair. "We are all responsible," my colleague the Right Reverend Eugene T. Sutton, bishop of the Episcopal Diocese of Maryland, insists as the Episcopal Church takes up the issue of reparations for our complicity in chattel slavery and white supremacy. As we do, we must accept backlash into the equation of our work and persevere. We do not choose where we are in the human story, only how we live in the time we are given.

There are spiritual parallels to the realities of letdown, payback, and backlash. For in every religious tradition, a high premium is placed, rightfully so, on mountaintop experiences, those moments that offer perspective and vision for our lives, when we feel what we can only describe as the palpable presence of God, or a sense of the sacred, however we name it.

For some, the conscious life of faith begins with such a moment, often referred to as a conversion experience. It can be a wake-up call of epic proportions, feeling oneself unconditionally loved, rescued from disaster, forgiven for past mistakes, and enabled to start over. For others, their spiritual consciousness has a far less dramatic beginning, with no one defining experience but instead a gradual sense of being led or inspired to live within a certain faith tradition or to open themselves to the mystery of the divine.

Either way, all those called to a life of faith come to rely upon those spiritual experiences and moments of illumination that give our lives meaning and direction. Without them, faith is reduced to a set of obligations to meet and rules to follow, or worse, a theological framework that only reinforces our own views and inclinations. Thus, a core spiritual practice of every tradition is to schedule periodic times away—on retreat or pilgrimage or a good vacation—so that we might set aside daily concerns and more fully open ourselves to the presence of God. We're encouraged to see ourselves through God's eyes and to trust that we are here on this earth to fulfill a unique vocation or destiny. At times, that sense of God's closeness and love is so strong that we lose, for a time, all sense of doubt, and we feel an abiding connection to sacred mystery, joy for the gift of our life, and clarity about our purpose for being.

Yet much of the spiritual life—as life in general—is lived not on the mountain, but in the valley, when the sense of God's presence is far less dramatic, if we sense God's presence at all. The challenge then is to trust that whatever vision or grace that was given to us was real, even when its emotional intensity fades, along with our confidence. Particularly jarring are the first few days after a transformational encounter or experience, when it seemed as if everything in our life was poised to change for the better, only to find ourselves back where we were before it happened, feeling the homeostatic pressure to fall into line.

For the past several years, I have sought the counsel of a wise Jesuit priest, Bill Kelly, whenever I feel the need to speak with someone farther along the spiritual path than I. He listens to my life's struggles with empathy and kindness and then offers bits of wisdom from the tradition in Roman Catholicism known as Ignatian spirituality, named for the sixteenth-century Spanish founder of the Jesuit order, Ignatius of Loyola. Among the most helpful has been St. Ignatius's understanding of the interplay between what he called experiences of spiritual consolation and desolation.

As the words imply, spiritual consolation comes to us in moments of intense joy or beauty, feelings of well-being and life purpose, of love or forgiveness. They are all wonderful in themselves, and they also can be the means through which we experience the love of God. Spiritual desolation, in contrast, is the opposite: those times of discouragement, apathy, heartbreak, and suffering that are not only difficult to endure but also cause us to question the validity of what we thought were our "spiritual experiences" and the presence, or very existence, of God.

To be sure, moments of consolation are what make the spiritual life worth living, and St. Ignatius was adamant that they are available to all people, not just those among the priestly class or other spiritual elites. As Jesuit Timothy Gallagher writes in *The Discernment of Spirits: An Ignatian Guide for Everyday Living,* "Consolation is not a remote mystical phenomenon beyond the comprehension of all but a few, but the way God is *ordinarily* encountered by human beings."[16]

Times of desolation are also universal, and from St. Ignatius's perspective, require deeper understanding and exploration than generally afforded or discussed among people of faith. Desolation is not merely going through a hard time; it's as if the spiritual lights of our lives go out completely. In a time of desolation, everything that once gave us confidence of God's love and presence collapses beneath us, or in a less-dramatic form, we don't feel anything at all. Like other forms of letdown, desolation causes us to doubt the validity of our uplifting and inspired moments of consolation.

The resources available to us in desolation are ones we all recognize: the empathy and solidarity of a good friend, the solace of nature, the small blessings of daily life, and the mercies of sleep. In the Ignatian tradition, we are discouraged from making life-altering decisions in desolation. As hard as it is, this is time, if possible, to persevere in small, life-affirming acts and tend to our souls with gentleness and grace—or just to hang on, in whatever ways we can. St. Ignatius would encourage us to hold fast to the memory of times of consolation and do our best to live as if they were true, even when we have lost confidence in them.

A key insight from Ignatian spirituality is that the feelings associated with *both* consolation and desolation are instructive, but they are not constant, nor does one reflect reality more than the other. Acknowledging this makes it easier to experience our emotions for what they are, allow them to wash over us, and let them go. We become less impressed by the feelings associated with consolation and less swayed by the feelings of desolation when they overtake us. "The ongoing alteration of these two movements is a normal pattern of every spiritual life," writes Gallagher.

> *Neither spiritual consolation nor spiritual desolation last forever; each will eventually give way to the other. Having experienced spiritual consolation, we are not to be surprised that spiritual desolation should arise once more; and when we are in spiritual desolation we should think ahead to the inevitable return of spiritual consolation, thus depriving the present desolation of much of its power.*[17]

Or the words of the Psalmist, "Weeping may linger for the night, but joy comes with the morning."[18]

In *Rising Strong*, Brené Brown describes the inevitable letdown and disorientation following the spiritual and creative energy she feels at the beginning of a creative process as "Day Two." Every time her team leads a three-day intensive training program for social workers and other professionals, she states: "No matter how many times we've done it and how many people we've certified, day two of this three-day model still sucks."[19] People are weary on the second day, the way forward unclear, and they've lost confidence in the inspiration they felt at the beginning.

In any creative process, what author and entrepreneur Scott Belsky coined as "The Messy Middle" is the hardest stretch. We're tired now, and the path ahead is anything but clear. Chaos is everywhere, and we are sorely tempted to quit. As Belsky set out to write a book dedicated to that middle space, he assumed that he would have plenty to share from his own experience of starting a new business. "But I couldn't remember anything," he confesses. "It wasn't memory loss—it was all just a blur."[20] He had to retrace his steps by reviewing old emails and screenshots he had taken on his phone of the mistakes and missteps along the way. Unless we take the time to honor and understand those stumbles and false starts, he warns, we risk celebrating others' successes without appreciating what was edited out or passed over in their life story. "What's in the middle?" he asks. "Nothing headline-worthy yet everything important":

> *Your war with self-doubt, a roller coaster of incremental successes and failures, bouts of the mundane, and sheer anonymity. The middle is seldom recounted and all blends together in a blur of exhaustion. We're left with shallow versions of the truth, edited for egos and sound bites. Success is misattributed to the*

moments we wish to remember rather than those we choose to forget. Worst of all, when everyone else around us perpetuates the myth of a straightforward progression from start to finish, we come to expect that our journey is meant to look the same. We're left with the misconception that a successful journey is logical. But it never is.[21]

A final example of letdown: As I mentioned in Chapter Three, for ten years I worked as a conference leader for Episcopal clergy for an organization known as CREDO. The goal for every gathering was for participants to come away with renewed vision and clarified goals for their ministries. Our task on the leadership team was to establish optimal conditions for participants to have mountaintop experiences of lasting value, enabling our world-weary colleagues a chance to rest, take stock, and dream boldly once again.

The first five days were rich with content from health professionals, financial and vocational advisers, and spiritual directors. Attendees came prepared to take a hard but loving look at their overall well-being, to affirm strengths and identify vulnerabilities, and to imagine a preferred future for their lives. The last three days were more like a retreat, with everyone invited to go deep within themselves and remember the courageous aspirations that inspired them to pursue ordained ministry in the first place. At the end, they wrote a document, called a CREDO plan, to capture all the insights they had and what they felt inspired to do going forward as a result.

As part of the required reading material for the conference, we gave the clergy a leadership article by Jim Collins and Jerry Porras titled "Building Your Company's Vision." The authors describe the relationship between core values, purpose, and competencies; the enduring character of one's identity; and the catalytic power of a "big, hairy, audacious goal," known as a BHAG.[22] A BHAG, I would explain, is a clear, compelling catalyst for change that begins a creative process, and a journey marked by courage and the willingness to take risks. Accomplishing a BHAG requires collaboration with others and at least ten years of hard and sustained work. There are no guarantees of success. Yet even naming such a future vision had a powerful effect; we could see it in the participants' eyes as they gave voice to what had been given them. But then we would all go home—back to our real lives, with all their stressors and competing demands.

I would sometimes run into participants at later church gatherings. As if they were case studies in letdown, almost everyone confessed to disappointment in themselves for not being able to fulfill what they had set their sights on. What's more, I knew exactly how they felt, for I had the same experience when I first attended a CREDO conference just months before my own leadership hopes were dashed.

I did my best to offer a word of encouragement to the clergy I met, commiserating with them about the difficulty of trusting the validity of our dreams when the reality of life takes over. "Don't give up," I would say, as much to myself as to them. "What you experienced and gave voice to when we were together was real. Dare to trust it even when you can't feel it anymore."

I realized that I needed to end our conferences with a frank conversation about reentry and the inevitability of letdown as something to factor in even as we're still on the mountaintop, looking off toward our preferred future. I made it my practice to refer back to the end of the article by Collins and Porras on vision, where they argue that success in any endeavor, paraphrasing Einstein's definition of genius, is 1 percent vision and 99 percent *alignment.*[23]

The work of alignment is never easy, almost always messy, and may well evoke resistance in those around us and even backlash from the wider society. It will most certainly involve long stretches when nothing much seems to be happening. There will be times of desolation, calling into question everything we experienced on our proverbial mountain. But as Brené Brown, Scott Belsky, and Ignatius of Loyola all teach us, the middle way is non-negotiable. Moreover, it doesn't get easier, no matter how many times you go through it. "Experience and success don't give you easy passage," Brown writes. "They only grant you a little grace, grace that whispers, 'this is part of the process. Stay the course . . . the middle is messy, but it's also where the magic happens.'"[24]

As I was packing up my desk in Minnesota in preparation for our move to Washington, D.C., I found my own CREDO plan, written thirteen years before, in the back of a desk drawer. I could never have guessed then how my life would unfold, nor how I would understand in a new way what I had once believed about my future and had come to doubt. "Dare to believe you are called to leadership," I had written. In the letdown that followed, I not only felt disappointment but also shame. How dare I imagine such a thing? Eventually, the path of preparation and skill-building presented itself, and I had to learn once again how to live and lead in the slow lane. The valley—when it comes to us in desolation, or a Day Two, or the messy middle, or payback or societal backlash—is where we cultivate, among other things, the virtue of perseverance.

CHAPTER SEVEN

The Hidden Virtue of Perseverance

And when you get down to it . . .
that's the only purpose grand enough for a human life.
Not just to love—but to persist in love.

—Sue Monk Kidd[1]

Madeleine Korbel Albright served as secretary of state from 1997 to 2001, the first woman to hold that position. Even a cursory summary of Albright's professional accomplishments could fill pages, yet she begins her memoir *Madam Secretary: A Memoir* acknowledging the implausibility of her career. An immigrant from Czechoslovakia, the mother of three children, she was almost forty years old before she held her first position in government. "Well into adulthood, I was never supposed to become what I became," she writes. "But if I had a late start, I also hurried to catch up."[2]

Catch up she did, building upon the foundation of an upbringing well suited for international diplomacy. She was the eldest child of a diplomat who was forced to leave Czechoslovakia with his family twice, first to England when the Nazis invaded in 1939, and again to the United States in 1948 when communists aligned with the Soviet Union took control of the country. By the time she was a teenager, Albright was fluent in Czech, French, and English. As a student at Wellesley College, she aspired to be a journalist. In the years devoted to furthering her husband's career and raising their children, she studied Russian and began a PhD.

Alongside her studies, she did the kind of volunteer work expected of women in Washington, D.C.: fundraising, serving on boards, volunteering at polling stations, and hosting international guests. She simultaneously relished the day-to-day tasks of motherhood, from sewing costumes to carpooling and helping her daughters sell Girl Scout cookies. Although in retrospect it may look like she always had her sights set on the highest levels of diplomacy and politics, her lived experience was different. "My life felt like a jigsaw puzzle," she acknowledges, "only I was working with several pieces from several puzzles simultaneously and there was no finished picture to tell me how it should all end up."[3]

Albright died on Wednesday, March 23, 2022, and in preparation for officiating at her funeral at Washington National Cathedral, I spent several weeks reading her memoirs. It felt like taking a master class in life and leadership. At the funeral, President Joseph R. Biden and former president Bill Clinton spoke in superlatives about her career. Former Secretary of State Hillary Clinton told stories of her brilliance, wit, and style. Her three daughters gave witness to her fierce love. Albright's memoirs touched upon all these elements of her life, but what struck me most was her perseverance. She did not make light of her struggles; she was aware of both her strengths and her vulnerabilities, and she readily admitted her mistakes. "Lives are necessarily untidy and uneven," she writes. "It is important, however, to have some guiding star. For me, that star has always been faith in the democratic promise that each person should be able to go as far as his or her talents will allow."[4]

She had worked hard to become, as Senator Barbara Mikulski described her in 1992, a "twenty-five-year overnight success."[5] As with all those whose lives we admire, much of that work was hidden from view: rising at 4:30 each morning to work on her dissertation, working for weeks behind the scenes before an event, mastering new languages and the complexities of global politics, and picking herself up after making a costly mistake, losing a political battle, or, most devastating, when her husband asked for a divorce.

In another memoir, *Prague Winter: A Personal Story of Remembrance and War, 1937–1948*, Albright explores the Jewish heritage that her parents kept from her and the cataclysmic events of her childhood, including the deaths of three grandparents in Nazi concentration camps. She doesn't hesitate to describe these lived experiences of cruelty, betrayal, and dreadful choices made in desperation, but she also declares, "they are not what I will take with me as I move to life's next chapter. In the world where I choose to live, even the coldest winter must yield to agents of spring and the darkest view of human nature must eventually find room for shafts of light."[6] She concludes with an ode to perseverance:

I have spent a lifetime looking for remedies for all manner of life's problems—personal, social, political, global. . . . I believe that we can recognize truth when we see it, just not at first and not without ever relenting in our effort to know more. This is because the goal we see, and the good we hope for, comes not as a final reward but as the hidden companion to our quest. It is not what we find, but the reason we cannot stop looking and striving that tells us why we are here.[7]

Perseverance is the hidden virtue of every courageous life. Rarely do we see what it costs others to do what seems effortless to us. Nor do we know what it took for them to carry on when they were tired or discouraged or to start again after failure or disappointment. Wherever we find ourselves in relation to the decisive moments that set us on our life's trajectory, perseverance is what enables us to keep going, even when we're stumbling in the dark.

Some people have a natural gift for perseverance. I know for certain that I do not, because I've had to learn it. As a child, I would watch my peers do what seemed to come easily to them, and when I couldn't do the same, I quit trying. I had modest aptitude in music and sports, but I never excelled in anything because I didn't know how to practice and fail, over and over, until crossing a threshold to a new level of competence. Somehow I managed to get through high school and into a decent college by running away from every academic discipline that intimidated me. In college, I panicked because there was so much that I didn't know how to do. For the first time in my life, I worked hard to keep up with my accomplished classmates—my first attempt at perseverance. But because I had such a poor academic foundation, I worked long hours with little to show for my efforts. It would take me an entire semester to write a ten-page paper.

You could say that I got through college on perseverance alone, if you define perseverance simply as effort, which I know now to be too narrow a definition. It wasn't until I began graduate studies in seminary that I learned the rudiments of writing. In my first year, a classmate who would become a lifelong friend, Linda Kaufman, sat me down and taught me the skills that I later watched my own children master in eighth grade. Linda was the first person to explain to me how to approach a body of information, organize my thoughts, write a first draft, and keep revising it. With her help, I wrote four ten-page papers in one semester. It felt like a miracle.

Still, the die was cast by my haphazard academic upbringing. There remain to this day considerable gaps in my knowledge base and weaknesses in my approach to accomplishing a task, academic or otherwise. I've learned how to persevere with intention, but mostly I still lean on the intuitive side of my brain that I've relied on all my life. It's a messy process and takes far longer than the end results suggest, but unlike in my childhood and adolescence, I know now to persevere when things are hard.

My formative lessons about perseverance in leadership came with the call to serve as rector of St. John's in Minneapolis. At age thirty-three, I could not believe my good fortune—not merely because I needed to get out of the church in Toledo, but more astonishingly, because St. John's was the church of my dreams, a community filled with energy, joy, and passion for justice. The move to Minneapolis was a leap of faith for our family, particularly for Paul, who had to leave a teaching job he loved. "Churches like St. John's don't come along every day," he said, laying down his own career for mine. "You have to say yes."

Then the church of my dreams became the struggle of my waking hours. Yes, the members were plucky, strong-willed, and proud of their outward focus and the journey back from near closure to becoming a destination congregation for young adults and families raising children. But it didn't take long to realize that the infrastructure upon which the life of the community depended was far more fragile than anyone realized. The initiatives that St. John's took the most pride in were sustained by a handful of people. There was conflict among the leadership that no one wanted to talk about, and a generational shift poised to occur but with a key generation missing due to the dramatic change of direction that the church had taken twenty years earlier. The building was in shabby condition, particularly in the areas devoted to children's education, and the pipe organ that the congregation had spent a lot of money to purchase a few years earlier was on its last legs. Other big maintenance issues were looming, and the annual budget was tight.

Thus, my leadership would not be defined by the bold, prophetic ministry I had imagined, but rather the largely invisible task of tending to a small and struggling institution. Nor did the congregation respond to me in the way I expected. They were proud of their decision to call a woman with two young children as their priest, yet few in authority were ready to allow me to lead. Most of my early suggestions were ignored.

I had a few decisive moments at St. John's in those years, but they were rare. Mostly it was the slow, steady effort of building

trust, setting an inviting tone in worship, fixing a leaking roof, re-
cruiting volunteers, trying my best to inspire in the pulpit each
week, making mistakes, learning from them, and starting again. In
the beginning, it took every bit of effort I had to remain calm and
focused when things weren't going as I had hoped. Moreover, Paul
was having trouble finding steady work. As I watched him struggle,
I worried that the price I asked him to pay for my dreams was too
high. The only thing that kept me going on the many days I felt
overwhelmed was how strongly I felt called to the work and Paul's
unwavering sense that things would work out.

I had only been there four months when we completed the annual ingathering of financial commitments necessary to draft the
church's budget for the coming year. Congregational response to
our requests for support had been tepid, and we were far short of the
resources needed to meet expenses, including my salary. If this was
a referendum on my leadership, I was failing.

Trying not to panic, I reached out to a member of the bishop's
staff, Howard Anderson, who was in charge of fundraising initiatives. "Gather up all your documents and come to my office," he
said, and for several hours we sat at a table as he helped me strategize a customized approach for each household of the congregation
whose commitment we had not yet received. Howard taught me
that raising money would be essential for the congregation to thrive,
as uncomfortable as it could be to solicit. "Money evokes all manner
of anxiety," he reassured me. "Don't take it personally when people
don't respond to financial appeals. Talking about money and raising
it is part of your job. If you do it steadily, with transparency, ac-
countability, and a vision for ministry, you'll be fine."

In this and similar moments, I learned that perseverance in leadership involved rolling up my sleeves and doing the very thing I didn't want to do. Every year, I still dreaded the financial pledge campaign, but I gave it my best effort so that we had the resources to do our ministry well. The capital campaigns, when we had to raise significant funds to renovate the century-old building, were even harder.

As in academics, perseverance in leadership isn't simply a matter of trying hard; there are disciplines, theoretical frameworks, and bodies of material to master. I already had some sense of this before I left Toledo. As I navigated my former boss's inappropriate and at times mean-spirited comments in those years, I noticed how his caustic moods and erratic behavior reverberated through the entire congregation, even among those untouched by his more egregious acts. It dawned on me that overall damage to the community was worse than his behavior toward me, for it was being held hostage by his poor leadership, and like a family with an alcoholic parent, he had inordinate control over its emotional sense of well-being.

At the suggestion of a friend, I read a book on congregational leadership by Rabbi Edwin Friedman titled *Generation to Generation: Family Process in Church and Synagogue.* It was revelatory. In the second chapter I came upon a passage describing the adverse effects of secrecy that took my breath away:

> *Family secrets act as the plaque in the arteries of communication....*
> *They create unnecessary estrangements as well as false compan-*
> *ionship. Secrets distort perceptions; members become confused or*
> *misled by information they obtain because they are seeing only*

part of the picture. The most important effect of secrets is that they
exacerbate other problems unrelated to the content of the secret
because they function to keep anxiety at high levels.[8]

Friedman was describing Trinity Church. I didn't know what
our secrets were, but evidence of them was everywhere. I also knew
that I needed help. I mustered up my courage and called Friedman
to ask if I could join one of his seminars for clergy. He wasn't recep-
tive, as groups had already been formed, and he suggested that I
apply for the following year. I pressed harder: "Is there any way I
might start sooner?" He was quiet for a moment and then asked,
sounding slightly irritated, "Have you read my book?" "I'm reading
it now," I replied. "Do you understand it?" "Yes," I lied. A month
later, I found myself traveling to Bethesda on a journey I would take
twice a year for the next decade.

Rabbi Friedman taught me, alongside an entire generation of
clergy, a theoretical framework that held out the possibility of
building a healthy, fruitful, and integrated leader. He argued that
this wasn't merely an appealing way for us to live, but essential to
the health of our whole community, because an organization can
only rise to the health and maturity of the people who lead it.
Maintaining such a life requires continual work of self-definition
and self-regulation in the context of relationships in three arenas:
your family of origin, your immediate family, and the dynamics of
the congregations you serve. Not just that, but all three are related,
so unresolved issues in one realm can produce symptoms in another. That awareness was enough to keep me in relationship with
my father and two stepmothers when it would have been easier to

drift away, and to work with Paul at the daily tasks of parenting well, which were not in conflict with my work, but were an integral part of it.

Regarding my plight as Walter Sobol's assistant, Friedman was blunt: "Get out of there as soon as you can," he said. "There's nothing you can do in your position except get in the way of what needs to happen between the congregation and its leader." I didn't want to believe him, but it soon became evident that he was right. As soon as I announced that I was leaving Trinity Church, the lay leaders took matters into their own hands.

In Minneapolis, I did my best to live and lead by the principles that Friedman taught. He and members of his faculty encouraged me to build a repertoire of specialized skills, so that, for example, I could deal with conflict directly or indirectly, depending on the situation. They encouraged me to lead transparently, acknowledging what I didn't know without ever feigning weakness to make others feel more powerful. They gave me practical tools to lower anxiety, deal with resistance, and learn from those who disagreed with me. I failed as often as I succeeded in these endeavors, but in failure as much as in success, I learned how to persevere.

Friedman also believed that an essential characteristic of leadership is having a spirit of adventure. The safest place for ships is the harbor, he'd say, but that's not what ships are for. Equally critical is persistence. He was fond of reminding us that no one has ever contributed significantly to the evolution of our species by working a forty-hour week. Still another characteristic is resilience. As the saying goes, he would remind us with a smile, no good deed goes unpunished.[9]

When I received word of Friedman's premature death in 1996, I sobbed in Paul's arms. How would I continue without him as a ballast in my life? Soon afterward, however, I had a sensation that I can only describe as a blessing, as if Friedman's spirit was assuring me that if I kept the posture of a student of leadership, I would be fine.

In a posthumously published book, *A Failure of Nerve: Leadership in the Age of the Quick Fix,* Friedman writes:

> *A leader is someone who has clarity about his or her own life goals, and is, therefore, someone who is less likely to become lost in the anxious emotional process swirling about. A leader is someone who can be separate while remaining connected, and therefore can maintain a modifying, non-anxious, and sometimes challenging presence. A leader can manage his or her reactivity to the automatic reactivity of others, and therefore be able to take a stand at the risk of displeasing others. It is not as though some leaders can do this and some cannot. No one does this easily, and most leaders, I have learned, can improve their capacity.[10]*

Friedman was always quick to say that leadership skills are beneficial for everyone, from parents to presidents, because they allow us to navigate well the realms of authority entrusted to us and create environments where others can thrive. These are the building blocks of sound relationships and a democratic society. Improving our capacity to lead, wherever we find ourselves, is a lifelong quest. With open hearts and minds, we can learn from anyone, and everyone around us benefits when we embrace the leadership that is ours.

I continued my studies with Friedman's faculty for a few more years, until I realized that I needed to augment what they had taught me with other leadership skills. I had become involved with a group of leaders in the Diocese of Minnesota who wanted to address the precipitous decline in membership and participation in all our congregations. Together we began to study the models of leadership in the fast-growing evangelical churches in Minnesota and across the country. I attended seminars led by prominent evangelical Christian leaders, and from them I learned compelling strategies to bring back to my own church. I was welcomed warmly by those whom I assumed, given our opposing positions in the culture wars, would have nothing but disdain for a leader of a small mainline denominational church. Their teaching led me to other sources, both religious and secular, and a course of study on congregational leadership that culminated in my Doctor of Ministry degree in 2008.

One theoretical framework in particular has greatly informed my understanding of how to lead a community through systemic change—the ultimate test in perseverance. In sociology, the theory is called the "diffusion of innovations," taken from the title of a groundbreaking book originally published in 1961 by Everett M. Rogers. Diffusion of innovation theory helps explain how, why, and how quickly large groups of people come to accept new ideas. It offers both a strategy for engagement and a means to overcome the natural human resistance to change.

Rogers studied the diffusion of innovations in multiple fields, including the introduction of hybrid seed corn among farmers in Iowa, basic hygiene practices in rural villages of Peru, the use of safety belts in automobiles, and the passing of anti-smoking legislation in the United States. He came to understand diffusion as a complex process in which an innovation is communicated over time among members of a group or organization and gradually adopted by those members in stages.[11] "An individual's decision is not an instantaneous act," he writes. "Rather it is a process that occurs over time and consists of a number of different actions."[12] Rogers outlines the necessary steps of decision-making and adoption of change, beginning when an individual or group is first exposed to an idea and concluding with its widespread acceptance. Although straightforward in the abstract, the process is rarely smooth and is fiercely resisted at first. Later, however, when the innovation has become normative, collective amnesia sets in about that initial resistance, particularly among those who fought hard to prevent its adoption! The outcome is never certain, but when systemic change occurs, it is because all the steps in the process of change have been taken.[13]

Rogers describes the ways in which different people relate to an innovation, according to their relationships within the social system and personal comfort level with the change proposed. They include the following:

1. *The Innovators*, who love both innovation and change. They play an essential role in launching the new idea into the system.

2. *The Early Adopters*, who are more integrated into the local system than the innovators, with the capacity to influence the opinions of others. They are respected by their peers and

ease communal uncertainty about a new idea when they adopt it.

3. *The Early Majority*, who assimilate a new idea only after the early adopters. Their position between the very early and the relatively late to embrace it make them an important link in the process.

4. *The Late Majority*, who adopt new ideas reluctantly, approaching all innovations with skepticism. They are influenced mostly by peer pressure and building momentum.

5. *Laggards*, who are the last to come along, if at all. Their resistance is strong and vocal, but in the end, they lack the capacity to influence others in rejecting the change. Some laggards will choose to leave the community or group rather than adapt to the new reality.

The fruitful practice of leadership requires an accurate assessment of where people are along this continuum and includes efforts to build momentum slowly through relationships and trust, for each category plays a key role in the diffusion process. The innovators, of course, are crucial, but without the support of the key influencers, their vision will not take root. In fact, innovators often leave when their ideas aren't adopted quickly enough because their greater commitment is to their vision, not the group. The work of the key influencers is to test judiciously what the innovators propose because only when they see it as trustworthy will they convince others to join them in acceptance.[14]

When the early majority is supportive, momentum shifts in favor of innovation. With his blockbuster *The Tipping Point: How Little Things Can Make a Big Difference*, author Malcolm Gladwell introduced to popular culture the ideas of threshold and critical mass.[15] As a tipping point is approached, just a few more people can suddenly make an enormous difference, and the rate of adoption then rapidly escalates.[16] Business author Jim Collins describes the same phenomenon in *Good to Great: Why Some Companies Make the Leap . . . and Others Don't*, in a section titled "Buildup and Breakthrough."[17] At a seemingly magical moment, the hard, steady work to produce a desired outcome crosses a threshold, and the same effort that produced little now yields fantastic results.

There is also a mystical, spiritual dimension to crossing the threshold of change that for leaders of faith like me feels like the power of the Holy Spirit. For when we reach what the Apostle Paul called the "acceptable time,"[18] or what Greek philosophers referred to as *kairos*, or "opportune time," things happen with ease and momentum, and in retrospect, seeming inevitability. Such moments, however, are built on countless other moments of invisible toil.

Learning diffusion of innovation theory was both a validation of my fledgling experience and a game changer for my leadership. It makes such sense and provides a road map for guiding a community through the process of change, whether it's a small congregation launching a capital campaign; the Diocese of Washington developing a strategic planning process for coming to terms with its racist past; or the society at large, as we grapple with the overwhelming realities before us, such as gun violence and climate change. It isn't enough to be right, or even to keep doing the same things repeatedly and expect things to transform. Hope, as they say, is not a strategy. Leadership requires the slow, steady work of building power through relationships and positioning ourselves to be most effective when the threshold moments come. As Rogers wrote in his book's opening sentence, "Getting a new idea adopted, even when it has obvious advantages, is difficult."[19]

There is also a heart component to perseverance, which Jesus emphasized when teaching his disciples about prayer. He did so by telling stories, such as one about a man who kept pounding on the door of a friend's house in the middle of the night demanding bread, and a widow who incessantly hounded a judge for the justice she deserved. These characters were hardly saints, as if to underscore that fact there is nothing visibly admirable about perseverance; they display only grit and dogged effort. According to the Gospel of Luke, Jesus told these parables to encourage his disciples to pray continually and not to *lose heart*.[20] He knew that life can be hard, and disappointments are real. Like Jesus' first disciples, we're bound to feel discouraged, and perseverance is what enables us to keep going until we find our footing again, so that we might connect to our heart energy and draw strength from it, even when there may be little to show for our efforts.

Yet simply trying hard doesn't serve us any better in prayer than in the rest of our lives, if it isn't tempered by a commitment to mindfulness and a willingness to learn some basic skills. Without them, perseverance in prayer can run amok, leading us down the path of magical thinking and the confusion of our desires with God's. We fall prey, in the words of the late Harvard Chaplain Peter Gomes, "to a false and phony version of the Christian faith that suggests that by our faith or our prayers we will be spared the burdens of life."[21] Thus perseverance in prayer isn't just about doing it more, but allowing our hearts to be stretched by the trials and struggles of life so that our capacity for love and forgiveness grows, as well as what we are willing to endure for the sake of love.

In a sermon Gomes preached at Harvard titled "Outer Turmoil, Inner Strength," he told the story of Ernest Gordon, for many years the chaplain at Princeton University and, more famously, the author of a memoir of his three-year captivity in a Japanese prison camp that was made into two films, *The Bridge on the River Kwai* and *To End All Wars*. Gomes recounted how Gordon and his fellow captives were initially very religious, "reading their Bibles, praying, singing hymns, witnessing and testifying to their faith, and hoping and expecting that God would reward them and fortify them for their faith by freeing them or at least mitigating their captivity."[22] Their suffering dragged on interminably, more among them died, and God did not deliver them as they had prayed. The men became understandably disillusioned and angry. They abandoned all their outward displays of piety and no longer expected God to save them.

But something else shifted for some of the men as they responded to the needs of their fellow prisoners, as they cared for and protected them and witnessed others sacrificing their lives in love. Quietly they began to speak about the presence of God in their midst. "This was not a revival of religion in the conventional sense," Gomes observed, "but rather the discovery that faith was not what you believed but what you did for others when it seemed you could do nothing at all."[23] Faith returned to them as the result of their compassion and, as they leaned into faith that God was with them in suffering, their capacity for compassion grew.

I wonder if God needs us to persevere in prayer simply because most of what we pray for will take a long time to realize. We pray for healing for ourselves and those we love, knowing that in most cases the process is slow. We pray for peace within our families or in the human family, and we know that peace isn't readily attained and often comes at a dreadfully high price. We pray for justice, knowing that it is always hard-won and takes generations to accomplish.

It was the American theologian Reinhold Niebuhr who wrote the words we now know as the Serenity Prayer: "God, grant me the serenity to accept the things I cannot change, the courage to change the things I can, and the wisdom to know the difference." Niebuhr himself was an extraordinarily persevering man. His generation of clergy began their ministries in the turbulent 1920s, struggling for workers' rights in an age of pervasive greed and disregard for the poor. He lived through the Great Depression, and he spoke against world complacency in the face of Hitler's rise to power. He persisted in writing, teaching, and preaching through the 1960s, when a series of strokes weakened him. He was arguably one of the most influential theologians of the mid-twentieth century, although he lived long enough to see his influence wane.

His daughter, Elisabeth Sifton, in a book honoring her father and his associates, writes: "They had both high spirits and serious, dedicated hearts. They worked so hard. They were so very loving.

And their labors were informed, in the end, by the humble recognition that it is not within our human powers to understand the final tally."[24] She concludes with my favorite Niebuhr quote, a call to perseverance:

> *Nothing worth doing can be achieved in a lifetime; therefore we must be saved by hope. Nothing that is true or beautiful or good makes complete sense in any immediate context of history; therefore we must be saved by faith. Nothing that we do, however virtuous, can be accomplished alone; therefore we are saved by love.*[25]

Intellectually, we may know that our most decisive moments are preceded by countless small decisions, invisible to others. Yet it's easy to lose sight of that truth as we slog through those stretches of preparation, trial and error, skill-building, and character formation. Perseverance is what keeps us going in the days without drama.

In her last book before her untimely death, the Christian writer Rachel Held Evans argued against the tendency in Christian theology to focus on Jesus' sacrificial death as if it was the sole purpose of life, reducing the Gospel to a transaction for the world's sins:

> *Jesus didn't just "come to die." Jesus came to live—to teach, to heal, to tell stories, to turn over tables, to touch people who weren't supposed to be touched and eat with people who weren't supposed to be eaten with. To break bread, to pour wine, to wash feet, to face temptation, to tick off the authorities, to fulfill Scripture, to announce the start of a brand-new kingdom, to show us what*

that kingdom is like, to show us what God is like, to love his en-
emies to the point of death at their hand, and to beat death by
rising from the grave.[26]

Jesus' cross was one he took up daily, and so must we. Our acts
of daily faithfulness and perseverance are part of a larger arc of
courage and resilience through which the power and the grace of
God are at work. The stories we tell and the moments we remember
may be about the decisive moments, but what matters most is how
those moments inform the living of each hour.

I conclude with one last story from Rachel Naomi Remen.
When she was five years old, she lived with her parents in a small
apartment in New York City. Her grandfather would often come to
visit, bearing gifts.

One day he brought her a small paper cup. She looked inside,
hoping to find something sweet to eat, but all the cup contained was
dirt. Her grandfather smiled at her disappointed face, brought her
into the kitchen, and put the paper cup on the window ledge. "If you
promise to put a little bit of water in the cup every day, something
special may happen," he said. It made no sense to her, but she promised her grandfather that she would, and she did.

At first, she wrote, it was easy to tend to this daily chore, as she
was curious to see what would happen. But as days went by and
nothing changed, remembering was harder. When her grandfather
returned a week later, she asked if it was time to stop. He said no.
By the second week, she felt angry and frustrated. When her grandfather came to visit, she wanted to give back the cup. But he refused
to take it: "Every day, Rachel, a bit of water." By the third week, she

often didn't think of her cup until she was in bed at night. Out of respect for her grandfather, she would get up and tend to her chore.

One morning, there were two little green leaves sprouting up from the dirt that had not been there the day before. She was astonished. Day by day, the plants grew a bit bigger. She couldn't wait to show her grandfather, whom she thought would be as amazed as she was. Instead, he explained to her that life is everywhere, and blessings are everywhere, hidden in the most ordinary and unlikely places. "And all it needs is water, Grandpa?" Rachel asked. "No," he said. "All it needs is your *faithfulness*."[27]

To persevere in faithfulness is our greatest gift to this world. The most influential moments in our lives and in human history depend far more than we realize on our faithfulness in small things, as we rise each day, like Rachel, and put a little water in our cup.

EPILOGUE

The brave man is not he who does not feel afraid,
but he who conquers that fear.

—Nelson Mandela[1]

To this day, people still approach me in the supermarket, at church conferences, or while I'm walking through my neighborhood, wanting to talk about the day former president Donald Trump held a Bible outside St. John's Church. Whenever I am introduced at a public event, my response to his actions is mentioned, as if it were the most noteworthy event in my ordained ministry. In these pages, I've sought to place the events of June 1, 2020, within a larger context, exploring how we learn to be brave over the course of a lifetime, and in all aspects of life, especially when the courageous decisions we make are known only to God.

Now in my seventh decade, I think a lot about how to speak of the challenges of our time with honesty, but not despair, with a sober assessment of the problems we face, and still with genuine hope for our future as a nation and a species. It isn't easy, for the divisions in our country have only deepened since President Trump left office in January 2021. Meanwhile, on the global stage, there are wars in many lands, large-scale migration on nearly every continent, and an ecological crisis imperiling the future of all humankind.

What I keep coming back to, as a source of hope and strength, are the historical accounts of men and women who faced the challenges of their times with grit and grace, the timeless stories of our spiritual and literary traditions that embody courage for us all, the people in my life whose courage and sacrificial love I admire, and the moments I have felt summoned to do what felt impossible at the time. Sometimes I succeeded; often I failed. But what seems to matter most in those moments is that we show up, step up, and make our offering despite its limitations and our own.

I'm equally inspired by the rising generation of leaders to whom the future belongs. Driving to church one Sunday morning, I caught the end of a podcast conversation between Krista Tippett, host of *On Being*, and Ayana Elizabeth Johnson, a marine biologist dedicated to addressing the global climate crisis. Johnson is the editor of an anthology titled *All We Can Save: Truth, Courage, and Solutions for the Climate Crisis*; cocreator of the podcast *How to Save a Planet*; and cofounder of the All We Can Save Project.

From the sound of these titles, you might surmise that Johnson is a naturally hopeful person, but she describes herself more as one drawn to solutions and getting things done. "I'm not a fan of hope as a guiding principle, because it assumes that the outcome will be good, which is not a given," she said. "But I am completely enamored with the amount of *possibility* that's available to us."[2]

My heart leapt when Johnson spoke of the possibility of our

getting things right, that we already have much of what we need to address climate change and other environmental concerns. "We just have to do it," she said. I found myself wondering, in how many other areas of life is it also true that we already have the solutions we need at our fingertips?

Johnson's rejection of a simplistic hope based on wishful thinking is, in fact, very close to the Christian understanding of what hope is—the capacity to face reality, no matter how difficult, and still seek whatever good is possible. As a person of faith, I dare to trust that God is at work amid the most challenging realities of our lives, and that by grace and acceptance, we join God in the holy work of transforming the world. Although I know that God cannot spare us from the consequences of our actions, I hold on to the promise that God will be with us always, to the end of the age. Moreover, I believe that God summons us to work together, as Bishop Barber said, in coalitions of the faithful, for the promise of a better day. Alone, we cannot accomplish anything worth doing. Still, it matters that we show up to do our part.

"This is a moment that calls for many leaders," Johnson said, "because what we need is transformation in every community, in every sector of the economy, in every ecosystem, with the hundreds of solutions we have.... It's all about how we build a future that we want to live in, where there's a place for us and the people and the things that we love."[3]

In every realm of life, in every country of the world, there are people who choose to be actively engaged to create the future Johnson believes is still possible. They are inspiring to be around because they are themselves inspired and motivated by love. But they are not in a class by themselves—we, too, can join them, and in fact we do, far more than we realize.

––––––––––

I wrote this book to honor the breadth and depth of what courage looks like in decisive moments, whether we are called upon to start, to go out and step up in public, or to stay put and persevere. All require great courage. In the words of David Whyte,

> *Courage is the measure of our heartfelt participation with life, with another, with a community, a work, a future. To be courageous is not necessarily to go anywhere or do anything except to make conscious those things we already feel deeply and then to live through the unending vulnerabilities of those consequences. To be courageous is to stay close to the way we are made.*[4]

My prayer is that, by grace, we all will be emboldened to lean into the wisdom, strength, power, and grace that come to us, whenever we find ourselves at a decisive moment. May you and I dare to believe that we are where we are meant to be when that moment comes, doing the work that is ours to do, fully present to our lives. For it is in this work that we learn to be brave.

ACKNOWLEDGMENTS

This book would never have been written were it not for Jennifer Gates and Catharine Strong of Aevitas Creative Management, who reached out to me in the summer of 2020 and encouraged me to begin. With warmth and patience, they guided me through the painstaking process of turning ideas into an outline and, from there, a proposal.

I'd like to thank Nina Shield, my editor at Avery, for her wisdom, thoughtful suggestions, and kindness. Thanks as well to Hannah Steigmeyer, who stepped in while Nina was on maternity leave and kept me on task. I was honored to work with them and all the team at Avery. Two angels along the way were Kem Meyer and Beth Graybill, both wonderful partners in creativity and women of deep faith. Margaret Shannon came in toward the end to help track down citations and permissions. She, too, was a godsend.

Special thanks to my friend and colleague Kelly Brown Douglas for suggesting that I include Pauli Murray and Howard Thurman in the book. Over dinner one evening when we were going to talk about Pauli, I asked Kelly about her life. Within minutes I knew that hers was a story that also needed to be told.

I feel the same about those whose courage I've done my best to describe. Some were new to me, discovered during my writing. Others I've carried with me for years. All their stories are sacred, and I pray that I've done them justice.

Heartfelt thanks to my family, friends, and colleagues who listened as I thought aloud about each chapter and allowed me the time and space to write. You are my inspiration and my joy.

Nearly every Sunday of my adult life, I rise to speak to a community of believers gathered to pray, reflect on sacred stories, and be open to the spirit of Jesus in our midst. Preaching is my spiritual practice. It is also a sacred conversation that continues well beyond the pulpit. Countless people have been my teachers and inspiration. This book is a distillation of what I've learned and have come to believe in Christian community. The errors in fact and perception are mine. The rest is amazing grace.

NOTES

1. Harry Emerson Fosdick (1878–1969) wrote the text "God of grace and God of glory" for the dedication of New York City's Riverside Church in 1930.

Lafayette Square—June 1, 2020

1. Remarks by the president of the United States, White House Rose Garden, Office of the White House Press Secretary.
2. The military leaders, mortified to realize they were being used as props in this staged photo-op, slipped away from the scene and soon publicly apologized. "I should not have been there. My presence in that moment and in that environment created a perception of the military involved in domestic politics," said General Mark Milley, chairman of the Joint Chiefs of Staff, in a keynote address to the National Defense Academy.
3. On August 24, 1814, as the War of 1812 raged on, invading British troops marched into Washington and set fire to the U.S. Capitol, the President's Mansion, and other local landmarks.
4. Designed by Benjamin Henry Latrobe, St. John's Church was consecrated on December 27, 1816.
5. Budde to CNN's Anderson Cooper.

Introduction

1. James Russell Lowell (1819–1891), "The Present Crisis," *The Boston Courier* (December 11, 1845). Lowell wrote the poem, at the request of John Greenleaf Whittier, as a protest against the annexation of Texas as a slave state.
2. Remarks by the Reverend Dr. William J. Barber II used by permission.
3. Ecclesiastes 3.1.

Notes

Chapter One: Deciding to Go

1. The life and work of Joseph Campbell (1904–1987) is largely responsible for our understanding of the hero's journey in ancient mythology, world religions, and popular culture. See *The Hero with a Thousand Faces (The Collected Works of Joseph Campbell)* (Novato, California: New World Library, 2008).

2. Henri Nouwen, *Bread for the Journey: A Daybook of Wisdom and Faith* (New York: HarperOne, 2006), entry for February 23.

3. Bruce Feiler, *Life Is in the Transitions: Mastering Change at Any Age* (New York: Penguin Press, 2020).

4. Walter Brueggemann, *Genesis: Interpretation: A Biblical Commentary for Teaching and Preaching* (Atlanta: John Knox Press, 1982), 105.

5. Genesis 12:1–4.

6. Genesis 18:12.

7. Bruce Feiler, *Abraham: A Journey to the Heart of Three Faiths* (HarperCollins e-books, 2002), 44.

8. Campbell, *The Hero with a Thousand Faces*, 18.

9. Joseph Campbell, *The Power of Myth with Bill Moyers*, ed. Betty Sue Flowers (New York: Doubleday, 1988), 124.

10. Henri Nouwen, *The Selfless Way of Christ: Downward Mobility and the Spiritual Life* (Maryknoll, New York: Orbis Books, 2007), 29.

11. Peter Eisenstadt, *Against the Hounds of Hell: A Life of Howard Thurman* (Charlottesville: University of Virginia Press, 2021), 206.

12. Howard Thurman, *With Head and Heart: The Autobiography of Howard Thurman* (San Diego: Harcourt Brace & Company, 1979), 20.

13. Thurman, *With Head and Heart*, 10.

14. Eisenstadt, 46.

15. Howard Thurman often wrote of the interplay between fate and destiny and the mysterious presence of God that encouraged him to live boldly. One example is found in his collection of weekly meditations from his years at the Church of the Fellowship, *Deep Is the Hunger* (New York: Harper & Row, 1951), 42–43.

16. Eisenstadt, 7.

17. Quoted in Eisenstadt, 21.

18. Thurman, *With Head and Heart*, 140.

19. Eisenstadt, 207–08.

20. Eisenstadt, 208.

Notes

Chapter Two: Deciding to Stay

1. On October 31, 1517, Martin Luther posted his 95 theses on the door of All Saints Church of Wittenberg, Saxony. Hauled before the Diet of Worms in April 1521 on allegations of heresy, he defended his actions: "I cannot and will not recant, because acting against one's conscience is neither safe nor sound. Here I stand; I can do no other. God help me."
2. Anne Tyler, *Saint Maybe* (New York: Alfred A. Knopf, 1991), 213.
3. Antoine de Saint-Exupéry, *The Little Prince* (New York: Harcourt, Brace & World, 1971), 77–87.
4. Frederick Buechner, *Listening to Your Life: Daily Meditations with Frederick Buechner* (New York: HarperCollins, 1992), 1.
5. Psalm 1:3.
6. Joan Chittister, *The Rule of St. Benedict: Insight for the Ages* (Chestnut Ridge, New York: Crossroad Publishing Company, 1992).
7. Chittister, *The Rule of St. Benedict*, 21–31.
8. John 6:60–68.
9. For a deeper reflection on the importance of tending to our faith, see Brian McLaren's wonderful book *Finding Our Way Again: The Return of the Ancient Practices* (Nashville: Thomas Nelson, 2010).
10. Kelly Brown Douglas, *What's Faith Got to Do with It? Black Bodies/Christian Souls* (Maryknoll, New York: Orbis Books, 2005), 53, Kindle.
11. Kelly Brown Douglas, "How Do We Know Black Lives Matter to God?" *The Christian Century*, September 30, 2020, https://www.christiancentury.org/article/how-my-mind-has-changed/how-do-we-know-black-lives-matter-god.
12. Douglas, "How Do We Know Black Lives Matter to God?"
13. Kelly Brown Douglas, *Resurrection Hope: A Future Where Black Lives Matter* (Maryknoll, New York: Orbis Books, 2021), xii.
14. Douglas, *Resurrection Hope*, 221.
15. Kati Marton, *Hidden Power: Presidential Marriages That Shaped Our Recent History* (New York: Pantheon Books, 2001), Chapter 2, 74, Kindle.
16. See especially Hazel Rowley's description in *Franklin and Eleanor: An Extraordinary Marriage* (New York: Picador, 2010), 39–63.
17. David Michaelis, *Eleanor* (New York: Simon & Schuster, 2020), 96.
18. Michaelis, 141.
19. Doris Kearns Goodwin, *No Ordinary Time: Franklin and Eleanor Roosevelt: The Home Front in World War II* (New York: Simon & Schuster, 1994), 19.

20. Blanche Wiesen Cook, *Eleanor: Volume One, 1884–1933* (New York: Penguin Books, 1992), 250.

21. Marton, *Hidden Power,* 894.

22. Goodwin, 11.

23. Thurman, *With Head and Heart,* 141.

Chapter Three: Deciding to Start

1. Chinese proverb ascribed to Laozi, Chapter 64, Dao De Jing.

2. Luke 9:35.

3. Luke 9:51.

4. "EL Doctorow in Quotes: 15 of His Best," *The Guardian,* July 22, 2015, https://www.theguardian.com/books/2015/jul/22/el-doctorow-in-quotes-15-of-his-best.

5. David Whyte, "Sweet Darkness," from *The House of Belonging* (1997) and *Essentials* (2020). Reprinted with permission from Many Rivers Press, Langley, Washington, https://davidwhyte.com.

6. Juan Williams, *Thurgood Marshall: American Revolutionary* (New York: Three Rivers Press, 1998), 89, Kindle.

7. Oliver Allen, "Chief Counsel for Equality," *Life* (June 13, 1955), 141, quoted in Williams, *Thurgood Marshall,* 1230.

8. Williams, 1307, Kindle.

9. Williams, 1307, Kindle.

10. Williams, 1311, Kindle.

11. Gilbert King, *Devil in the Grove: Thurgood Marshall, the Groveland Boys, and the Dawn of a New America* (New York: Harper Perennial, 2012), 2.

12. King, *Devil in the Grove,* 360.

13. Pauli Murray, *Song in a Weary Throat: An American Pilgrimage* (New York: Liveright Publishing, 2012), 124.

14. Murray, 237.

15. Troy R. Saxby, *Pauli Murray: A Personal and Political Life* (Chapel Hill: University of North Carolina Press, 2020), 110, Kindle.

16. Rosalind Rosenberg, *Jane Crow: The Life of Pauli Murray* (New York: Oxford University Press, 2017), 116, Kindle.

17. Rosenberg, 187.

Chapter Four: Accepting What You Do Not Choose

1. American theologian Reinhold Niebuhr reportedly wrote the prayer in

1932–1933. See Elizabeth Sifton, *The Serenity Prayer: Faith and Politics in Times of Peace and War* (New York: W. W. Norton & Company, 2003), 289.

2. "God of Grace and God of Glory," Hymn #584, *The Hymnal 1982* (New York: Church Publishing, 1982).

3. J. R. R. Tolkien, *The Lord of the Rings: The Fellowship of the Ring*, Second Edition (Boston: Houghton Mifflin, 1954), 50.

4. Ronald A. Heifetz and Marty Linsky, *Leadership on the Line: Staying Alive through the Dangers of Leading* (Boston: Harvard Business School Press, 2002), 13.

5. Dietrich Bonhoeffer, *Gesammelte Schriften* [*Collected Writings*], ed. Ebhard Bethge, I:320 (Munich: Haiser, 1958).

6. Quoted in *Strange Glory: A Life of Dietrich Bonhoeffer* by Charles Marsh (New York: Alfred A. Knopf, 2014), 342, Kindle.

7. Romans 5:3–5.

8. Philippians 3:10.

9. Colossians 1:2.

10. 2 Corinthians 12:8–10.

11. Rachel Naomi Remen, MD, *Kitchen Table Wisdom: Stories That Heal*, 10th Anniversary Edition (New York: Riverhead Books, 2006), xxxvii, Kindle.

12. Remen, *Kitchen Table Wisdom*, 29, Kindle.

13. Remen, *Kitchen Table Wisdom*, 29, Kindle.

14. Remen, *Kitchen Table Wisdom*, 30, Kindle.

15. Remen, *Kitchen Table Wisdom*, 17, Kindle.

16. Rachel Naomi Remen, MD, *My Grandfather's Blessings: Stories of Strength, Refuge, and Belonging* (New York: Riverhead Books, 2000), 29.

17. Matthew 26:39.

18. Isaiah 42:6–7.

19. Isaiah 53:45.

20. Isaiah 53:10–11.

21. Romans 3:23–25.

22. Rachel Held Evans, *Inspired: Slaying Dragons, Walking on Water, and Loving the Bible Again* (Nashville: Thomas Nelson, 2018), 155, Kindle.

23. Colossians 1:19.

24. John 1:5.

25. Kate Bowler, *Everything Happens for a Reason: And Other Lies I've Loved* (New York: Random House, 2018), xvi, Kindle.

26. Michael K. Honey, *Going Down Jericho Road: The Memphis Strike, Martin Luther King's Last Campaign* (New York: W. W. Norton & Company, 2007), 26–27.

27. Mika Edmondson, *The Power of Unearned Suffering: The Roots and Implications of Martin Luther King, Jr.'s Theodicy* (Lanham, Michigan: Lexington Books, 2007), xi.

28. Martin Luther King Jr., *Stride Toward Freedom: The Montgomery Story* (New York: HarperCollins, 1987), 224, cited in Edmondson, 16.

29. Martin Luther King Jr., "Pilgrimage to Nonviolence," in *The Christian Century* (April 13, 1960), 439–41, included in James M. Washington, ed., *A Testament of Hope: The Essential Writings and Speeches of Martin Luther King, Jr.* (San Francisco: HarperSanFrancisco, 1986), 40.

30. Martin Luther King Jr., "Suffering and Faith," cited in Washington, 43.

31. King Jr., "Suffering and Faith," in Washington, 43.

32. Honey, 97.

33. Joseph Rosenbloom, *Redemption: Martin Luther King's Last 31 Hours* (Boston: Beacon Press, 2018), 32.

34. Rosenbloom, 36.

35. Honey, 428.

36. Honey, 452.

37. Honey, 381.

38. Honey, 381.

39. Taylor Branch, *At Canaan's Edge: America in the King Years, 1965–68* (New York: Simon & Schuster, 2006), 756.

40. Martin Luther King Jr., "I See the Promised Land," in Washington, 28.

41. King Jr., "I See the Promised Land," in Washington, 286.

42. Martin Luther King Jr., "Remaining Awake through a Great Revolution," in Washington, 272–73.

43. King Jr., "I See the Promised Land," in Washington, 285.

44. James H. Cone, *The Cross and the Lynching Tree* (Maryknoll, New York: Orbis Books, 2011), 85, 87.

45. Michael Curry, *Love Is the Way: Holding on to Hope in Troubling Times* (New York: Avery, 2020), 27.

Chapter Five: Stepping Up to the Plate

1. Gregory Boyle, *Barking to the Choir: The Power of Radical Kinship* (New York: Simon & Schuster, 2017), 29, Kindle.

2. I began using the phrase "stepping up to the plate" in sermons to describe what we were all called to do in a season of intense need. Because I sometimes preach in Spanish, I wondered how it translated. It doesn't. There is, however, a close

parallel expression from the Castilian sport of bullfighting: *coger el toro por los cuernos*, that is, "to take the bull by the horns." I came across another saying in Spanish that didn't quite cut it, but nonetheless made me smile: *ponerle el cascabel al gato*. As an expression, it means to have the courage to do what others dare not. In English, it means "to put a bell on a cat."

3. Luke 4:18–19.

4. Luke 4:21.

5. John 18:28–38.

6. Michael Curry, *The Power of Love: Sermons, Reflections, and Wisdom to Uplift and Inspire* (New York: Avery, 2018), 8.

7. Curry, *The Power of Love*, 11.

8. Isaiah 6:5.

9. Luke 5:8.

10. 2 Corinthians 4:7.

11. Mark 6:36.

12. John 6:12.

13. James Clear, "What Every Successful Person Knows, But Never Says," James Clear, December 14, 2015, https://jamesclear.com/ira-glass-failure.

14. Clear, "What Every Successful Person Knows."

15. Brené Brown, *Rising Strong: How the Ability to Reset Transforms the Way We Live, Love, Parent, and Lead* (New York: Random House, 2017), loc. 202, Kindle.

16. Brown, 274, Kindle.

17. Brown, 958, Kindle.

18. Brown, 3594, Kindle.

19. Curry, *Love Is the Way*, 181.

20. Brown, 3605.

21. Genesis 31:3.

22. Genesis 32:26–28.

23. Justin Welby, sermon preached at Washington National Cathedral, September 27, 2020, https://cathedral.org/sermons/sermon-the-most-rev-justin-welby-archbishop-of-canterbury/.

24. Welby, sermon at Washington National Cathedral.

25. I tell Henry Caffey's story with Andrew Waldo's permission. I first heard Andrew tell the story in a sermon he preached on April 23, 2004.

26. Charles W. Eagles, *Outside Agitator: Jon Daniels and the Civil Rights Movement in Alabama* (Tuscaloosa: University of Alabama Press, 2000), 28.

27. Quoted in Eagles, 27.

28. Rich Wallace and Sandra Neil Wallace, *Blood Brother: Jonathan Daniels and His Sacrifice for Civil Rights* (Calkins Creek, 2016), 137, Kindle.

29. Stephanie Spellers, *The Church Cracked Open: Disruption, Decline, and New Hope for Beloved Community* (New York: Church Publishing, 2022), 81.

30. Wallace and Wallace, 225.

31. Eagles, 184.

32. Eagles, 168.

33. Eagles, 169.

Chapter Six: The Inevitable Letdown

1. Attributed to Oscar Wilde.

2. Mark 1:11–12.

3. Matthew 16:13–14.

4. Matthew 16:15–18.

5. Matthew 16:21–23.

6. See https://isaiahmn.org/ for more information about ISAIAH's work.

7. John 21:15–19.

8. David Paulsen, "Q&A: Washington Bishop Mariann Budde says Church Should 'Lead with Jesus' in Its Nonpartisan Advocacy," Episcopal News Service, February 4, 2021, https://www.episcopalnewsservice.org/2021/02/04/qa-washington -bishop-mariann-budde-says-churchs-nonpartisan-advocacy-should-lead-with -jesus/.

9. Brown, 200.

10. Lawrence B. Glickman, "How White Backlash Controls American Progress," *The Atlantic*, May 22, 2020, https://www.theatlantic.com/ideas/archive/2020 /05/white-backlash-nothing-new/611914/.

11. Ta-Nehisi Coates, *We Were Eight Years in Power: An American Tragedy* (New York: One World, 2017), xiii, Kindle.

12. Coates, 64.

13. Coates, 109.

14. Coates, 202.

15. Coates, 288.

16. Timothy M. Gallagher, OMV, *The Discernment of Spirits: An Ignatian Guide for Everyday Living* (New York: Crossroad Publishing Company, 2005), 57.

17. Gallagher, 110.

18. Psalm 30:5.

19. Brown, 630.
20. Scott Belsky, *The Messy Middle: Finding Your Way Through the Hardest and Most Crucial Part of Any Bold Venture* (New York: Portfolio/Penguin, 2018), 3, Kindle.
21. Belsky, 7, Kindle.
22. Jim Collins and Jerry I. Porras, "Building Your Company's Vision," *Harvard Business Review*, https://hbr.org/1996/09/building-your-companys-vision. Accessed August 17, 2022.
23. Collins and Porras.
24. Brown, 641.

Chapter Seven: The Hidden Virtue of Perseverance

1. Sue Monk Kidd, *The Secret Life of Bees* (New York: Viking, 2020), 289.
2. Madeleine Albright, *Madam Secretary: A Memoir* (New York: HarperCollins, 2003), 6, Kindle.
3. Albright, *Madam Secretary*, 89.
4. Albright, *Madam Secretary*, 10.
5. Albright, *Madam Secretary*, 6.
6. Madeleine Albright, *Prague Winter: A Personal Story of Remembrance and War, 1937–1948* (New York: HarperCollins, 2013), 414.
7. Albright, *Prague Winter*, 414.
8. Edwin H. Friedman, *Generation to Generation: Family Process in Church and Synagogue* (New York: Guilford Press, 1985), 52.
9. Friedman, *Generation to Generation*, 188.
10. Edwin H. Friedman, *A Failure of Nerve: Leadership in the Age of the Quick Fix* (New York: Seabury Books, 2007), 14.
11. Everett M. Rogers, *Diffusion of Innovations* (New York: Free Press, 1995), 5.
12. Rogers, 169.
13. Rogers, 11.
14. Rogers, 300.
15. Malcolm Gladwell, *The Tipping Point: How Little Things Can Make a Big Difference* (Boston: Little, Brown and Company, 2000), Kindle 12.
16. Gladwell, 13.
17. Jim Collins, *Good to Great: Why Some Companies Make the Leap . . . and Others Don't* (New York: HarperCollins, 2001), 165.
18. 2 Corinthians 6:2.
19. Rogers, 1.
20. Luke 18:1.

21. "Outer Turmoil, Inner Strength," by Peter J. Gomes, in *Strength for the Journey: Biblical Wisdom for Daily Living* (San Francisco: HarperSanFrancisco, 2003), 140.

22. Gomes, 148.

23. Gomes, 149.

24. Elisabeth Sifton, *The Serenity Prayer: Faith and Politics in Times of Peace and War* (New York: W. W. Norton & Company, 2003), 348.

25. Sifton, 349.

26. Rachel Held Evans, *Inspired: Slaying Giants, Walking on Water, and Loving the Bible Again* (Nashville: Thomas Nelson Books, 2018), 148, Kindle.

27. Remen, *My Grandfather's Blessings*, 1–2.

Epilogue

1. Nelson Mandela, *Long Walk to Freedom: The Autobiography of Nelson Mandela* (Boston: Little, Brown, 1994), 622, Kindle.

2. Anya Elizabeth Johnson, June 9, 2022, https://onbeing.org/programs/ayana-elizabeth-johnson-what-if-we-get-this-right/. Accessed August 16, 2022.

3. Johnson, https://onbeing.org/programs/ayana-elizabeth-johnson-what-if-we-get-this-right/.

4. David Whyte, *Consolations: The Solace, Nourishment and Underlying Meaning of Everyday Words* (Langley, Washington: Many Rivers Press, 2015), 224, Kindle.

BIBLIOGRAPHY

BOOKS

Albright, Madeleine. *Madam Secretary: A Memoir*. New York: HarperCollins, 2003.

Albright, Madeleine. *Prague Winter: A Personal Story of Remembrance and War, 1937–1948*. New York: HarperCollins, 2013.

Belsky, Scott. *The Messy Middle: Finding Your Way Through the Hardest and Most Crucial Part of Any Bold Venture*. New York: Portfolio/Penguin, 2018.

Bonhoeffer, Dietrich. *Gesammelte Schriften* [*Collected Writings*]. Edited by Ebhard Bethge, I:320 (Munich: Haiser, 1958).

Bowler, Kate. *Everything Happens for a Reason: And Other Lies I've Loved*. New York: Random House, 2018.

Boyle, Gregory. *Barking to the Choir: The Power of Radical Kinship*. New York: Simon & Schuster, 2017.

Branch, Taylor. *At Canaan's Edge: America in the King Years, 1965–68*. New York: Simon & Schuster, 2006.

Brown, Brené. *Rising Strong: How the Ability to Reset Transforms the Way We Live, Love, Parent, and Lead*. New York: Random House, 2017.

Brueggemann, Walter. *Genesis: Interpretation: A Biblical Commentary for Teaching and Preaching*. Atlanta: John Knox Press, 1982.

Buechner, Frederick. *Listening to Your Life: Daily Meditations with Frederick Buechner*. New York: HarperCollins, 1992.

Campbell, Joseph. *The Hero with a Thousand Faces (The Collected Works of Joseph Campbell)*. Novato, California: New World Library, 2008.

Campbell, Joseph. *The Power of Myth with Bill Moyers*. Edited by Betty Sue Flowers. New York: Doubleday, 1988.

Chittister, Joan. *The Rule of Benedict: Insights for the Ages*. Chestnut Ridge, New York: Crossroad Publishing Company, 1992.

Coates, Ta-Nehisi. *We Were Eight Years in Power: An American Tragedy.* New York: One World, 2017.

Collins, Jim. *Good to Great: Why Some Companies Make the Leap . . . and Others Don't.* New York: HarperCollins, 2001.

Cone, James H. *The Cross and the Lynching Tree.* Maryknoll, New York: Orbis Books, 2011.

Cook, Blanche Wiesen. *Eleanor: Volume One, 1884–1933.* New York: Penguin Books, 1992.

Curry, Michael, Bishop. *Love Is the Way: Holding on to Hope in Troubling Times.* New York: Avery, 2020.

Curry, Michael, Bishop. *The Power of Love: Sermons, Reflections, and Wisdom to Uplift and Inspire.* New York: Avery, 2018.

Douglas, Kelly Brown. *Resurrection Hope: A Future Where Black Lives Matter.* Maryknoll, New York: Orbis Books, 2021.

Douglas, Kelly Brown. *What's Faith Got to Do with It? Black Bodies/Christian Souls.* Maryknoll, New York: Orbis Books, 2005.

Eagles, Charles W. *Outside Agitator: Jon Daniels and the Civil Rights Movement in Alabama.* Tuscaloosa: University of Alabama Press, 2000.

Edmundson, Mika. *The Power of Unearned Suffering: The Roots and Implications of Martin Luther King, Jr.'s Theodicy.* Lanham, Michigan: Lexington Books, 2007.

Eisenstadt, Peter. *Against the Hounds of Hell: A Life of Howard Thurman.* Charlottesville: University of Virginia Press, 2021.

The Episcopal Church. *The Hymnal 1982.* New York: Church Publishing, 1982.

Evans, Rachel Held. *Inspired: Slaying Giants, Walking on Water, and Loving the Bible Again.* Nashville: Thomas Nelson, 2018.

Feiler, Bruce. *Abraham: A Journey to the Heart of Three Faiths.* New York: William Morrow, 2002.

Feiler, Bruce. *Life Is in the Transitions: Mastering Change at Any Age.* New York: Penguin Press, 2020.

Friedman, Edwin H. *A Failure of Nerve: Leadership in the Age of the Quick Fix.* New York: Seabury Books, 2007.

Friedman, Edwin H. *Generation to Generation: Family Process in Church and Synagogue* (The Guilford Family Therapy Series). New York: Guilford Press, 1985.

Gallagher, Timothy M. *The Discernment of Spirits: An Ignatian Guide for Everyday Living.* New York: Crossroad Publishing Company, 2005.

Gladwell, Malcolm. *The Tipping Point: How Little Things Can Make a Big Difference.* Boston: Little, Brown and Company, 2000.

Gomes, Peter J. *Strength for the Journey: Biblical Wisdom for Daily Living.* San Francisco: HarperSanFrancisco, 2003.

Goodwin, Doris Kearns. *No Ordinary Time: Franklin and Eleanor Roosevelt: The Home Front in World War II.* New York: Simon & Schuster, 1994.

Heifetz, Ronald A., and Marty Linsky. *Leadership on the Line: Staying Alive through the Dangers of Leading.* Boston: Harvard Business School Press, 2002.

Honey, Michael K. *Going Down Jericho Road: The Memphis Strike, Martin Luther King's Last Campaign.* New York: W. W. Norton & Company, 2007.

King, Gilbert. *Devil in the Grove: Thurgood Marshall, the Groveland Boys, and the Dawn of a New America.* New York: Harper Perennial, 2012.

King, Martin Luther, Jr. "Pilgrimage to Nonviolence," in *The Christian Century* (April 13, 1960). https://www.christiancentury.org/article/pilgrimage-nonviolence.

King, Martin Luther, Jr. *Stride Toward Freedom: The Montgomery Story.* New York: HarperCollins, 1987.

Marsh, Charles. *Strange Glory: A Life of Dietrich Bonhoeffer.* New York: Alfred A. Knopf, 2014.

Marton, Kati. *Hidden Power: Presidential Marriages That Shaped Our Recent History.* New York: Pantheon Books, 2001.

McLaren, Brian. *Finding Our Way Again: The Return of the Ancient Practices.* New York: Thomas Nelson, 2010.

Michaelis, David. *Eleanor.* New York: Simon & Schuster, 2020.

Murray, Pauli. *Song in a Weary Throat: An American Pilgrimage.* New York: HarperCollins, 1987.

Nouwen, Henri. *Bread for the Journey: A Daybook of Wisdom and Faith.* New York: HarperOne, 2006.

Nouwen, Henri. *The Selfless Way of Christ: Downward Mobility and the Spiritual Life.* Maryknoll, New York: Orbis Books, 2007.

Remen, Rachel Naomi, MD. *Kitchen Table Wisdom: Stories That Heal,* 10th Anniversary Edition. New York: Riverhead Books, 2006.

Remen, Rachel Naomi, MD. *My Grandfather's Blessings: Stories of Strength, Refuge, and Belonging.* New York: Riverhead Books, 2000.

Rogers, Everett M. *Diffusion of Innovations.* New York: Free Press, 1995.

Roosevelt, Eleanor. *You Learn by Living: Eleven Keys for a More Fulfilling Life.* New York: Harper, 1960.

Rosenberg, Rosalind. *Jane Crow: The Life of Pauli Murray.* New York: Oxford University Press, 2017.

Bibliography

Rosenbloom, Joseph. *Redemption: Martin Luther King's Last 31 Hours.* Boston: Beacon Press, 2018.

Rowley, Hazel. *Franklin and Eleanor: An Extraordinary Marriage.* New York: Picador, 2010.

Saint-Exupéry, Antoine de. *The Little Prince.* New York: Harcourt, Brace & World, 1971.

Saxby, Troy R. *Pauli Murray: A Personal and Political Life.* Chapel Hill: University of North Carolina Press, 2020.

Sifton, Elisabeth. *The Serenity Prayer: Faith and Politics in Times of Peace and War.* New York: W. W. Norton & Company, 2003.

Spellers, Stephanie. *The Church Cracked Open: Disruption, Decline, and New Hope for Beloved Community.* New York: Church Publishing, 2021.

Thurman, Howard. *Deep Is the Hunger.* New York: Harper & Row, 1951.

Thurman, Howard. *With Head and Heart: The Autobiography of Howard Thurman.* San Diego: Harcourt Brace & Company, 1979.

Tolkien, J. R. R. *The Lord of the Rings: The Fellowship of the Ring,* Second Edition. Boston: Houghton Mifflin, 1954.

Tyler, Anne. *Saint Maybe.* New York: Alfred A. Knopf, 1991.

Wallace, Rich, and Sandra Neil Wallace. *Blood Brother: Jonathan Daniels and His Sacrifice for Civil Rights.* Calkins Creek, 2016.

Washington, James M., ed. *A Testament of Hope: The Essential Writings and Speeches of Martin Luther King, Jr.* San Francisco: HarperSanFrancisco, 1986.

Whyte, David. *Consolations: The Solace, Nourishment and Underlying Meaning of Everyday Words.* Langley, Washington: Many Rivers Press, 2015.

Whyte, David. *The House of Belonging* and *Essentials.* Langley, Washington: Many Rivers Press, 1997 and 2020.

Williams, Juan. *Thurgood Marshall: American Revolutionary.* New York: Three Rivers Press, 1998.

WEBSITES

Clear, James. "What Every Successful Person Knows, But Never Says." Accessed June 10, 2022. https://jamesclear.com/ira-glass-failure.

Collins, Jim, and Jerry I. Porras. "Building Your Company's Vision." *Harvard Business Review.* September–October 1996. https://hbr.org/1996/09/building-your-companys-vision.

Douglas, Kelly Brown. "How Do We Know Black Lives Matter to God?" *The Christian Century.* September 30, 2020. https://www.christiancentury.org/article/how-my-mind-has-changed/how-do-we-know-black-lives-matter-god.

Bibliography

"EL Doctorow in Quotes: 15 of His Best." *The Guardian.* July 22, 2015. https://www
.theguardian.com/books/2015/jul/22/el-doctorow-in-quotes-15-of-his-best.

Glickman, Lawrence B. "How White Backlash Controls American Progress." *The
Atlantic.* May 22, 2020. https://www.theatlantic.com/ideas/archive/2020/05/white
-backlash-nothing-new/611914/.

Johnson, Ayana Elizabeth. "What If We Get This Right?" *On Being with Krista Tippett.* June 9, 2022. https://onbeing.org/programs/ayana-elizabeth-johnson-what
-if-we-get-this-right/.

Paulsen, David. "Q&A: Washington Bishop Mariann Budde Says Church Should 'Lead
with Jesus' in Its Nonpartisan Advocacy." Episcopal News Service. February 4,
2021. https://www.episcopalnewsservice.org/2021/02/04/qa-washington-bishop
-mariann-budde-says-churchs-nonpartisan-advocacy-should-lead-with-jesus/.

Welby, Justin. Sermon preached at Washington National Cathedral, September 27,
2020. https://cathedral.org/sermons/sermon-the-most-rev-justin-welby-arch
bishop-of-canterbury/.

PERMISSIONS ACKNOWLEDGMENTS